SpringerBriefs in Economics

Kobe University Social Science Research Series

The Kobe University Social Science Research Series has been established as a subseries of the SpringerBrief in Economics Series, but in fact this exciting interdisciplinary collection encompasses scholarly research not only in the economics but also in law, political science, business and management, accounting, international relations, and other subdisciplines within the social sciences. As a national university with a special strength in the social sciences, Kobe University actively promotes interdisciplinary research. This series is not limited only to research emerging from Kobe University's faculties of social sciences but also welcomes cross-disciplinary research that integrates studies in the arts and sciences.

Kobe University, founded in 1902, is the second oldest national higher education institution for commerce in Japan and is now a preeminent institution for social science research and education in the country. Currently, the social sciences section includes four faculties—Law, Economics, Business Administration, and International Cooperation Studies—and the Research Institute for Economics and Business Administration (RIEB). There are some 230-plus researchers who belong to these faculties and conduct joint research through the Center for Social Systems Innovation and the Organization for Advanced and Integrated Research, Kobe University.

This book series comprises academic works by researchers in the social sciences at Kobe University as well as their collaborators at affiliated institutions, Kobe University alumni and their colleagues, and renowned scholars from around the world who have worked with academic staff at Kobe University. Although traditionally the research of Japanese scholars has been publicized mainly in the Japanese language, Kobe University strives to promote publication and dissemination of works in English in order to further contribute to the global academic community.

More information about this series at http://www.springer.com/series/15423

Bishnu Kumar Adhikary
Kenji Kutsuna · Takaaki Hoda

Crowdfunding

Lessons from Japan's Approach

Springer

Bishnu Kumar Adhikary
Graduate School of Business Administration
Kobe University
Kobe, Hyogo, Japan

Takaaki Hoda
Graduate School of Business Administration
Kobe University
Kobe, Hyogo, Japan

Kenji Kutsuna
Graduate School of Science, Technology and Innovation
Kobe University
Kobe, Hyogo, Japan

ISSN 2191-5504 ISSN 2191-5512 (electronic)
SpringerBriefs in Economics
ISSN 2520-1697 ISSN 2520-1700 (electronic)
Kobe University Social Science Research Series
ISBN 978-981-13-1521-3 ISBN 978-981-13-1522-0 (eBook)
https://doi.org/10.1007/978-981-13-1522-0

Library of Congress Control Number: 2018947500

Printed on acid-free paper

This Springer imprint is published by the registered company Springer Nature Singapore Pte Ltd.
The registered company address is: 152 Beach Road, #21-01/04 Gateway East, Singapore 189721, Singapore

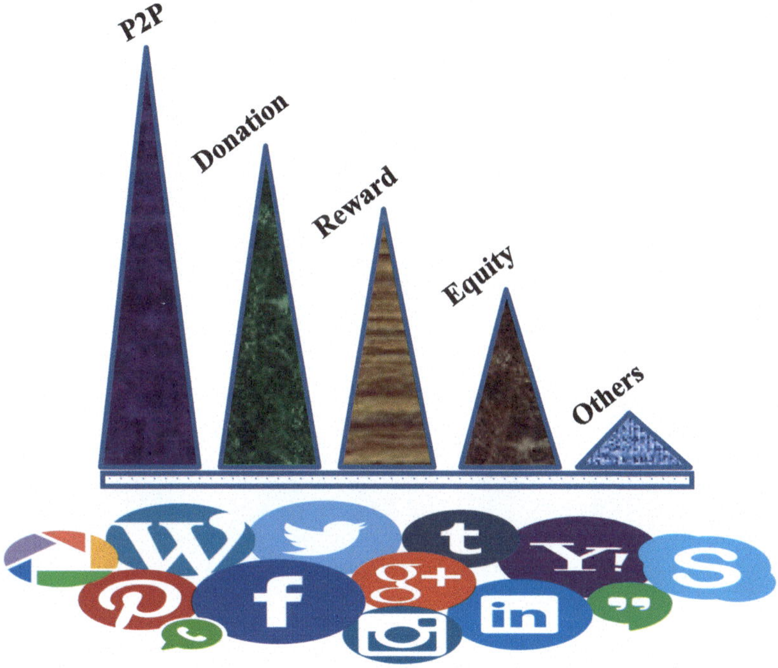
P2P
Donation
Reward
Equity
Others

Preface

Crowdfunding is a new market-based financial approach that leverages social media and information technology to intermediate finance to those are in need of it, startups and idea creators, in particular. Crowdfunding falls under the ambit of new entrepreneurial finance. Though at the initial stage, crowdfunding was used mainly for receiving a donation for a charitable purpose, the concept turned into a business idea in the wake of subprime mortgage crisis 2008 that caused commercial banks to adopt tighter lending policies to small and medium enterprises (SMEs) and startups.

With a slow introduction of crowdfunding in 2009 (US$0.53 billion), the industry grew to US$34.4 billion in 2015, reflecting a 103% growth rate on an average over this period. The industry expects to reach nearly US$187 billion including peer-to-peer (P2P) lending in 2021 (statistia.com, 2017), while the equity crowdfunding expects to reach $36 billion by 2020, likely to surpass the venture capital industry as a significant source of startups' finance (Barnet 2015). Now, crowdfunding is used to finance not only the startups and idea creators but also the matured industries such as real estate and construction firms.

Given the spectacular growth and direction of crowdfunding, this book reviews crowdfunding concepts, models, growth, and patterns with a particular focus on the activities of Japanese crowdfunding to help academics, researchers, and policy-making institutions.

This book is different from other books of crowdfunding in that it provides a separate chapter on the activities of crowdfunding in Japan by including a case of crowdfunding platform (Music Securities) and giving evidence of a crowdfund-backed firm (SABAR Restaurant). Importantly, unlike the Western crowdfunding models that are seemingly profit oriented with a short-term focus, Japan's crowdfunding models tend to be long term with a community approach backed by stakeholder theory, as it incorporates local banks and city officials in the lending models. Thus, knowledge of Japan's crowdfunding approach is indeed important for Asian economies to make the crowdfunding ecosystem vibrant, credible, and sustainable.

Another distinguishing feature of this book is that it explores crowdfunding potential for addressing the financial needs of startups and SMEs in developing countries considering Bangladesh as a case. The book discusses problems of the financial system of Bangladesh and argues that the principal financial actors such as the traditional banking system, stock markets, and non-government organizations (NGOs) tend to face a systematic problem to cater to the funding needs of the SMEs and the entrepreneurial firms, in particular. It presupposes that Bangladesh as a developing country indeed has the opportunity to build a crowdfunding ecosystem to give access to credits to the entrepreneurial firms and to leapfrog its capital market structure to the developed world. The book, then, studies socioeconomic dynamics and market readiness of Bangladesh with a view to introducing crowdfunding technology. It further discusses how to build a suitable crowdfunding ecosystem considering socioeconomic and cultural aspects of Bangladesh.

In addition, the book expects to help beginners interested in crowdfunding. In fact, the first three chapters (Chaps. 1–3) deliberate crowdfunding concepts, benefits, features, models, types, growth, and patterns to acquaint the beginners with the knowledge of crowdfunding industry.

Notably, the interest of academics, researchers, and policy-makers has not been left out. The last four chapters (Chaps. 4–7) are likely to shoot up their interest in crowdfunding. For instance, Chap. 4 reviews the prior literature on crowdfunding, which is limited but proliferating, to help find research gaps in this new phenomenon. This chapter also discusses some theories such as networking, signaling, stakeholder, and financial disruption that are likely to contribute to the development and diffusion of crowdfunding technology. It further highlights some issues for future research.

On the other hand, Chap. 5 unveils crowdfunding activities in Japan, and Chap. 6 explores crowdfunding potential for financing SMEs and entrepreneurial firms in developing countries such as Bangladesh. Chapters 5 and 6 expect to help researchers and policy-making institutions to design a suitable crowdfunding ecosystem. Finally, Chap. 7 identifies some lessons of crowdfunding to advance more research on this phenomenon and to make it efficient and sustainable. As a whole, the book expects to provide ample benefits to novices, academics, researchers, and policy-makers interested in crowdfunding technology.

Kobe, Japan Dr. Bishnu Kumar Adhikary
Kobe University

Acknowledgements

Writing a book is magnificent and challenging as well at the same time. To complete this book, we received ample supports and assistance directly and indirectly from many personalities that made this book a reality. Here, we express gratitude and thanks to all those people.

At the onset, we would like to express sincere gratitude and thanks to the JSPS committee members who reviewed and accepted our Grant-in-Aid research proposal, and the officials of the Ministry of Education, Culture, Sports, Science and Technology, Japan, for allocating funds to research crowdfunding. This book is the outcome of the Grant-in-Aid Research No. 15H03378.

We convey special thanks to Mr. Yusuke Tsujimoto, Former Ph.D. student of Kobe University, who participated in conducting interviews with Music Securities and SABAR Restaurant in Japan and subsequently translated Japanese documents into English. His contribution to this book is undoubtedly valuable.

We highly acknowledge the help and invaluable suggestions provided by Prof. Toufic Ahmad Choudhury, Director General of Bangladesh Institute of Bank Management (BIBM), Dhaka, in conducting interviews with the bank officials in Bangladesh. We also appreciate Mr. Golam Monowar Kamal, Former Managing Director of Bangladesh Venture Capital Limited (BVCL) for his constructive feedback in improving the quality of the book. We further extend thanks to Mr. Riton C. Paul, Assistant Professor of Government Azizul Haque College, Bogra, for assisting us in conducting interviews and collecting data from small business firms in Bogra. Many thanks are also due to Mr. Takanobu Migita, the owner of SABAR Restaurant, and officials of Music Securities for giving us an interview on their firms and sharing invaluable information.

We are indebted to some academics both in Japan and abroad for their suggestions and comments which we received from academic conferences and seminars. We are especially grateful to Prof. Suzuki Yasushi of Ritsumeikan Asia Pacific University, Japan; Dr. Sarkar Humayun Kabir of Taylors' University, Malaysia; and Prof. Mahfuzul Hoque, and Mizanur Rahman of Dhaka University,

Bangladesh, for making fruitful comments on our papers when presented at their academic seminars.

Last but not least, we are grateful to the staff of Kobe University research office, academic office, and accounting section, Ms. Aki Mukunoki, Ms. Masako Ohnishi, and Ms. Asahara Michiko, in particular, for their continuous support in preparing the documents for business trips and providing funds timely.

Contents

About the Authors

Bishnu Kumar Adhikary is Associate Professor at the Graduate School of Business Administration, Kobe University, Japan. He obtained an MBA (finance) and a Ph.D. from Ritsumeikan Asia Pacific University, Japan. He also earned an MBA (marketing) from Calcutta University, India, and an M.Com. (accounting) from the University of Dhaka, Bangladesh. He has publications at different reputed journals such as *Journal of Multinational Financial Management, Asia Pacific Business Review, Journal of Comparative Asian Development, South Asian Journal of Business Studies, and Contemporary South Asia.*

Kenji Kutsuna is Professor and Vice Dean of the Graduate School of Science, Technology and Innovation, Kobe University, Japan. He obtained a Ph.D. (commerce) from Osaka City University, Japan. He is also Professor of entrepreneurial finance at the Graduate School of Business Administration, Kobe University. His academic works have appeared in several high-ranked journals such as *Journal of Finance, Journal of Financial Economics, Review of Financial Studies, Journal of Banking and Finance, and Journal of Corporate Finance.*

Takaaki Hoda is Associate Professor responsible for corporate finance and entrepreneurial finance at the Graduate School of Business Administration, Kobe University, Japan. He is also Assistant Director of SESAMI Program at the Graduate School of Business Administration, Kobe University. He earned a Ph.D. (commerce) from Waseda University, Japan. His works appeared in several reputed journals such as *Venture Policy* and *Public Policy Review*.

Chapter 1
Crowdfunding—A Conceptual Talk

1.1 What Is Crowdfunding?

Crowdfunding can be defined as a practice of funding startups or small firms or a project by raising small amounts of money from a large number of people utilizing online social media such as Facebook, Twitter, LinkedIn and other specialized blogs. It is an organized collective effort of many non-professional people who are embedded in trust to finance a venture via the internet. It is a market-based approach to finance entrepreneurial firms that lack capital for growth and development. It is also known as social lending (Hulme and Wright 2006) and peer-to-peer (P2P) lending (Freedman and Jin 2008).

The term "Crowdfunding" is derived from another term "crowdsourcing" that refers to the process of obtaining needed services, assets, knowledge, or ideas by soliciting contributions from a large number of individuals, a crowd of people especially from the online community rather than from the traditional employees or suppliers. In the case of crowdfunding, the same process is followed in procuring funds. However, the objective of crowdfunding is to finance a project or an idea or to help a philanthropic organization by soliciting funds in a tiny unit from mass people. As Lambert and Schwienbacher (2010) note,

> Crowdfunding involves an open call, essentially through the internet, for the provision of financial resources either in the form of donations (without rewards) or in exchange for some form of reward and/or voting rights in order to support initiatives for specific purposes. [Lambert and Schwienbacher 2010, p. 6]

In fact, crowdfunding can be viewed as a by-product of information technology. This new form of financial technology emerged in the wake of 2008 financial meltdown in response to the increased difficulties faced by the small business entrepreneurs in obtaining funds from the traditional banking system. Its underlying foundation is rooted in the three factors: trust, internet technology, and willingness of the people. In addition to raising funds for the entrepreneurs, crowdfunding is

B. K. Adhikary et al., *Crowdfunding*, SpringerBriefs in Economics,
https://doi.org/10.1007/978-981-13-1522-0_1

a technique to validate entrepreneurial project by the potential user groups at the shortest possible time.

Notably, the traditional method of raising finance for a project includes preparation of a business plan, the undertaking of market research and then approaching wealthy individuals, banks, angel investors and venture capital firms limiting the fund raiser's option to a few key players. Crowdfunding, on the other hand, expands the fund raiser's reach and players as he can advertise his presence to a large number and variety of potential investors through the presence of online crowdfunding platforms or social media. Simultaneously, it helps fund suppliers to the reduction in transaction cost of investment by providing them opportunities to act as a quasi-monitor of the investee firms because the data on available investment opportunities and the reaction of other fund suppliers can be centrally accessed under the crowdfunding system.

1.2 Benefits of Crowdfunding

Crowdfunding allows the fundraiser to tap into a broader investor pool and provides him with more flexible fundraising options. Here are some of the benefits of crowdfunding:

Reach—A crowdfunding platform expands the fundraiser's reach by giving him access to thousands of accredited investors who can see, interact with and share the fundraiser's particular fundraising campaign.
Presentation—By creating a crowdfunding campaign, a fundraiser goes through the invaluable process of examining his business from every angle—its history, traction, offerings, addressable market, value proposition, and more thus summarising his business into a polished, attractive and easily understandable proposition.
Public Relation (PR) and Marketing—From its launch to its close, the fundraiser can share and promote his campaign through social media, email newsletters, and other online marketing channels. As the fundraiser and other media outlets cover the progress of the fundraiser, the fundraiser can further promote his business by steering traffic to his website and channelizing other company resources.
Validation of Concept—The presentation of his business to the masses provides an opportunity to the fundraiser to validate and refine his business proposition. Questions and expressions of interest from potential investors can make the fundraiser re-examine his business proposition to see whether he has missed out on something important which would make his investors more likely to offer money for his project.
Efficiency—Crowdfunding is an efficient way to organize one's business. In crowdfunding, an entrepreneur can centralize and streamline fundraising efforts by building a single comprehensive project profile to which he can direct all his potential investors thus eliminating the need to approach them individually. So, instead of duplicating efforts by printing documents, compiling binders, and manually updating each one when there's an update, the fundraiser can present everything online

in a much more accessible format, leaving him with more time to run his business instead of fundraising.

1.3 Evolution of Crowdfunding

Although Crowdfunding is only recently starting to capture global interest as an alternative investment vehicle, crowdfunding has been around in less conspicuous forms for hundreds of years. Whenever we put a few dollars in the offering plate at church, chip into fund a Christmas party for neighborhood children, or give to a charitable organization, we are effectively participating in crowdfunding. Notable examples of veritable crowd campaigns are the funding of the pedestal of the Statue of Liberty and the Empire State Building.

Modern-day crowdfunding, however, came into being in the 1990s when some platforms for charity fundraising and projects funded by Internet-based campaigns emerged into the forefront. The UK-based charity fundraising platform JustGiving was founded in the year 2000. Then, ArtistShare, a reward-based crowdfunding platform (CFP), was founded by Brian Camelio in 2000 with the idea that fans would finance production costs for albums sold only on the Internet and artists also would enjoy much more favorable contract terms. Other reward-based platforms continued to emerge. A well-known and heralded example was Sellaband, founded by Holland's Pim Betist in 2005. Sellaband's model allowed artists to build a fan base, receive contributions under a product presale model (in this case, a record album), and if the contribution level reached the target threshold, produce, market, and distribute albums.

In the year 2005, the first ever platform where entrepreneurs could lend money to develop their ideas was launched. This platform was called Kiva. Today, Kiva is one of the most successful micro-lending platforms all over the world. Kiva's success led to the mushrooming of more such peer to peer lending platforms like Zopa, Prosper, Lending Club and so on. Another popular crowdfunding platform Indiegogo came to be launched in the year 2008. Then, Kickstarter appeared within a year in 2009. Both these platforms are extremely preferred in the current crowdfunding market. The difference between these crowdfunding platforms and other crowdfunding platforms is that in these platforms the investors do not get their money back but instead receive rewards depending on the plan of the project owner.

Crowdfunding emerged as a business tool for financing the startups and small firms just after the 2008 financial meltdown that tightened, *inter alia*, the lending requirements of the commercial banks to startups and small and medium enterprises (SMEs). Many entrepreneurs have managed to survive this harsh period relying on various crowdfunding platforms. If we look at the present market scenario, the way forward for crowdfunding platforms seems to be extremely promising. Examples of some significant crowdfunding developments identified by Esposti (2013), the CEO of Massolution.com, are as follows:

Niche platforms—Niche industry and sector-specific platforms become apparent as crowdfunding is increasingly seeking more benefits from market differentiation. Reward-based crowdfunding platforms focus on video games, real estate, food and beverage, recording art, performing art, fashion, journalism, and so on to tap the benefits of servicing a common niche or industry. As Esposti (2013) notes "While it's smart for a new platform to choose a specific niche simply to differentiate its service, there is another big reason why this trend is likely to prevail—it helps build a repeated crowd on the platform. Having crowdfunders visit a platform, not just because they have been invited to a specific campaign, but because the campaigns appeal to their tastes, is extremely valuable".

Locavesting—Locavesting refers to investment in local enterprises that have potential to grow. In a book, "*Locavesting: The Revolution in Local Investing and How to Profit From it*" Cortese (2011) describes how local investing is emerging and that crowdfunding is boosting it. She argues that a small investment in locally-owned enterprises with the help of crowdfunding can generate tremendous economic and social benefits for individuals, their communities and the country as well. Rebirth Financial, a crowdfunding platform that provides business loans, focuses on locavesting and helps local entrepreneurs in getting funds for businesses.

Enterprise crowdfunding—Large enterprises and associations started leveraging the benefits of crowdfunding for their companies in some areas such as raising social profiles, market testing, and spin-ins of entrepreneurial ventures. The perceived benefit of enterprise crowdfunding is not only to raise less contractual funds for investment but also to shoot the enterprise's reasons for standing in society. Crowdfunding is now perceived as a new source of capital for commercial, residential, and infrastructure projects.

Crowdfunding economic development—In a report "*Crowdfunding's Potential for a Developing World*," the World Bank advocates crowdfunding tool to scale up the economic development of a country, the developing countries, in particular. According to World Bank (2013) areas such as solar energy, education, and urban development could be most promising for economic enhancement. To this tune, crowdfunding may work with micro-finance because both microfinance and crowdfunding intend to provide financial support to small businesses that have less access to it. Now, it is time to link crowdfunding with microfinance to advance development at the macro level.

Live crowdfunding—Live crowdfunding is a technique to tag investors hidden needs at the initiation of campaigns or expos. The objective of live crowdfunding is to increase media attention for crowds and trigger their interest in investment. Also, in this crowdfunding, anyone can lend funds right on the spot.

1.4 Features of Crowdfunding

Crowdfunding represents a revolution in how entrepreneurial ventures are funded and disrupts traditional financial flows. Critical features of crowdfunding are as follows.

(a) Crowdfunding takes advantage of the new features of the Web 2.0, especially viral networking and marketing and social media to collect funds from the masses within a relatively short time span.
(b) It helps suppliers of funds to reduce their transaction cost of investment and gives them the chance to act as quasi-monitors of the investee firms as data on available investment opportunities and reactions of others who are supplying funds can easily be tracked under one crowdfunding platform.
(c) The entrepreneurial firms can receive sufficient freedom in the use of funds as against traditional bank loans which involve contractual obligations in the use of funds.
(d) Crowdfunding or the "pennies from many models," as it is known, allows people to materialize their creative or entrepreneurial visions. It is an exciting way to gather attention, validate an idea, and most importantly, raise capital without going into debt.
(e) Crowdfunding promises to democratize and expand the access to capital by enabling the community that is, the crowd to determine which entrepreneurs (micro, small and medium-sized enterprises) can obtain funds for growth.
(f) By centralizing access to data on available investment opportunities, crowdfund-investing portals can facilitate the flow of information from early-stage enterprises to potential investors more rapidly than has ever been possible before.
(g) Crowdfunding allows investors to screen many proposals at one time and determine quickly whether the company fits their portfolio strategy, risk appetite, or other criteria.
(h) Crowdfunding is a boundary-less approach to investment. Therefore, geography is not a barrier to the funding of projects.
(i) Crowdfunding helps build exposure for the firms by receiving feedback from customers. Early-stage firms may use crowdfunding to explore the viability of products at a low cost with low barriers to entry. Extensive feedback from potential investors and customers help entrepreneurs to revise the business model.

1.5 Crowdfunding Concepts

One can have inventive crowdfunding ideas which could all be novel ways to raise funds for a variety of projects. Here are some crowdfunding concepts.

❖ ***Youngsters can crowdfund***

Crowdfunding can both help youngsters and get them involved in it. A site called Piggyback uses the crowdfunding model and applies it in a way that allows children to fund projects related to their education, whether it is a Science Fair, a Summer Camp or new school uniforms. This same platform can be used to raise funds for needy street children in developing countries to fund three basic meals a day and a basic education.

❖ ***Crowdfunding as a means to publish books***

Pubslush is a crowdfunding site that deals exclusively with aspiring authors and writers. Aspiring writers upload a summary and ten best pages of their book for the world to see. And the writers get to keep whatever amount they have collected even if it falls short of the goals they have set on the site.

❖ ***Crowdfunding as a way to reward honesty***

Crowdfunding can also be used to help people who help others. In September 2013, Glen James, a homeless man from Boston returned a backpack to the police which had $40,000 in traveler's cheques and $2400 in cash. The police then returned the backpack to its rightful owner. Virginia Resident Ethan Whittington was touched by Glen's honesty and decided to start a crowdfunding campaign to reward him using a platform called GoFundMe. At first, the goal of raising funds was $50,000 but donations continued to pour in quickly so that the target was raised to $250,000.

1.6 Crowdfunding Versus Microfinance

Crowdfunding is fundamentally different from Microfinance, which is a rule-based institutional credit given to poor women, in particular, in a tiny amount. A case in point is Grameen Bank, Bangladesh. It provides microfinance to the poor people in Bangladesh. Microcredit is primarily a phenomenon dependent on the microfinance institutions where the institutions are the sole originator, provider, and risk-taker of the loan. By contrast, crowdfunding is a market-based online financial tool where a large pool of investors jointly screens the viability of a project before committing final investment. Crowdfunding platforms help meeting borrowers and investors by creating an online platform. Unlike microfinance institutions that directly disburse credits, crowdfunding platforms facilitate financial transactions for a fee, and they seldom invest in the firms seeking capital through their platforms. Crowdfunding platforms do the primary screening of a proposal and conduct necessary campaigns for raising funds when it deems viable. This means that crowdfunding platforms just originate a loan and the suppliers of the fund, who are ordinary people, bear the risk of the fund.

Moreover, growth firms are in need of larger amounts of funds which cannot be gained through microcredit institutions, as it exceeds their funding limits. However, larger amounts of funds can be obtained through the power of social networks such as crowdfunding. It is here that crowdfunding fills the gap between microfinance and institutional investors and does not pose a threat to microfinance.

Crowdfunding is a boundary-less approach to investment, whereas geography constrains the suppliers and receivers of microcredits. In addition, in crowdfunding, many investors screen proposals at one time and provide feedback. Whereas, in microcredit, screening of proposals is first done by group members who plan to obtain credit and then examined by a loan officer from the microcredit institutions.

Crowdfunding can be used to test the validity of a product or to advertise products of a firm, but the primary purpose of microcredits is to generate income for poor people. However, crowdfunding extends some of the social mechanics of microfinance to help fund high-growth start-ups, frequently in the technology sector, or to provide expansion capital to existing businesses.

References

Cortese A (2011) Locavesting: the revolution in local investing and how to profit from it. Wiley, Hoboken

Esposti C (2013) 5 ways the booming crowdfunding ecosystem is changing in 2013. Retrieved April 15, 2017, from https://venturebeat.com/2013/05/22/5-ways-the-booming-crowdsourcing-ecosystem-is-changing-in-2013/

Freedman S, Jin G (2008) Do social networks solve information problems for peer-to-peer lending? Evidence from Prosper. Com. NET Institute Working Paper No. 08-4. Retrieved April 15, 2017, from http://www.nsd.edu.cn/cn/userfiles/Other/2010-/201005071421115167158l.pdf*

Hulme M, Wright C (2006) Internet-based social lending: past, present and future. Soc Futures Obs. Retrieved May 04, 2017 from http://www.socialfuturesobservatory.co.uk/pdf_download/internetbasedsociallending.pdf

Lambert T, Schwienbacher A (2010) An empirical analysis of crowdfunding. Retrieved May 04, 2017 from http://ssrn.com/abstract=1578175

World Bank (2013) Crowdfunding potentials for the developing world. *Info Dev*, Finance and Private Sector Development Department, Washington D.C.

Chapter 2
Crowdfunding—Types and Models

2.1 Types of Crowdfunding

Crowdfunding can be broadly categorized into two groups: community-based crowdfunding and financial return-based crowdfunding. Community-based crowdfunding can again be divided into a donation or perks-based crowdfunding (hereafter "donation-based") and reward-based crowdfunding. Likewise, financial return-based crowdfunding is divided into three categories: lending-based or peer-to-peer (P2P) lending crowdfunding (hereafter "lending-based"), equity-based crowdfunding, and royalty-based crowdfunding. Financial return-based crowdfunding is also known as security-based crowdfunding. Figure 2.1 identifies different types of crowdfunding.

Donation-based crowdfunding and reward-based crowdfunding are popularly used to raise funds for a philanthropic purpose or testing a product or ideas for future commercial use. For example, Nakedwines.com raised $10 million from angel investors in 2013 for the expansion into the US and Australia. Nakedwines.com has

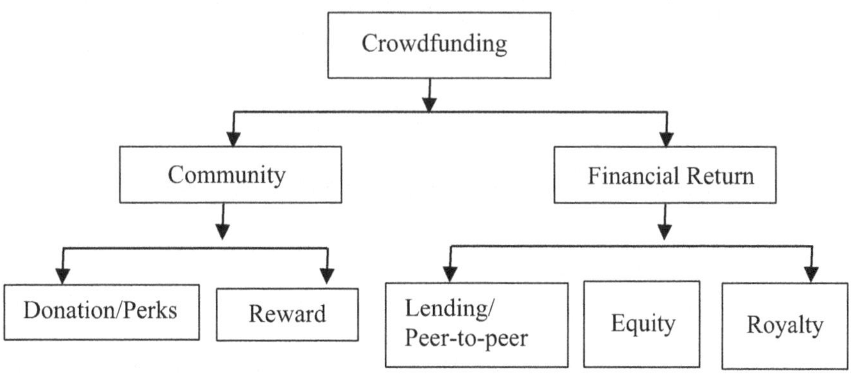

Fig. 2.1 Types of crowdfunding. *Source* Authors' construction

B. K. Adhikary et al., *Crowdfunding*, SpringerBriefs in Economics,
https://doi.org/10.1007/978-981-13-1522-0_2

nearly 150,000 angel investors who primarily fund independent winemakers in return for a 25–50% price of a wine's retail price (Shu 2013). Donation-based crowdfunding usually does not provide any financial return to the fund suppliers, whereas reward-based crowdfunding offers a token gift to the fund suppliers as appreciation. Leading donation-based crowdfunding platforms are Justgiving (UK), GoFundMe (USA), and Indiegogo (USA). Leading reward-based crowdfunding platforms are GoFundMe (USA), Kickstarter (USA), Indiegogo (USA), Ulule (France), and Fundrazr (Canada).

By contrast, the lending-based crowdfunding, equity-based crowdfunding, and royalty-based crowdfunding are used for a commercial motive to raise capital by selling financial instruments against firm's assets. In lending-based crowdfunding, fund suppliers receive a fixed interest and principal on maturity or a specified schedule. This type of crowdfunding is suitable for firms that have positive cash flows and is particularly important for the small firms in developing countries, as they face funding problem due to lack of institutional building. Leading lending-based crowdfunding platforms are LendingClub (USA), Prosper (USA), Ratesetter (UK), Zopa (UK), and Lufax (China).

On the other hand, fund suppliers under the equity-based crowdfunding receive dividends in the form of cash or equity or any profit sharing arrangement. This type of crowdfunding is suitable for the growth firms or firms in an expansion stage. Leading equity-based crowdfunding platforms are EquityNet (USA), Crowdfunder (USA), CrowdCube (UK), Angelist (USA), and OurCrowd (Israel). Notably, equity fund providers are ranked below the creditors because equity providers are regarded as residual claimants. Thus, equity crowdfunding may raise conflicts with the security laws in the traditional stock market. Hence, the application of equity crowdfunding requires additional or more complex security laws.

The royalty-based crowdfunding provides fund suppliers a percentage or a fixed amount of the revenue system. This is similar to the technology patenting or licensing. The royalty fees are distributed to fund suppliers on a pro-rata basis to their investment amount. In addition to the anchored crowdfunding models, there are also hybrid crowdfunding models—a model that encompasses both lending and equity characteristics. However, the hybrid crowdfunding models are complex and not frequently used by fundraisers.

2.2 Crowdfunding in a Funding Life Cycle of a Firm

Figure 2.2 identifies the place where crowdfunding fits into the funding life cycle of a growth firm. According to Fig. 2.2, startups in a seed stage are a better candidate for donation or perks-based crowdfunding. When the firm reaches the early stage and flourishes, the equity-based or lending-based crowdfunding becomes suitable for meeting the funding needs. In this time, the royalty-based crowdfunding can also be made. Notably, crowdfunding does not replace the venture capitalists or angel investors instead it serves as a compliment for them, indicating that all of

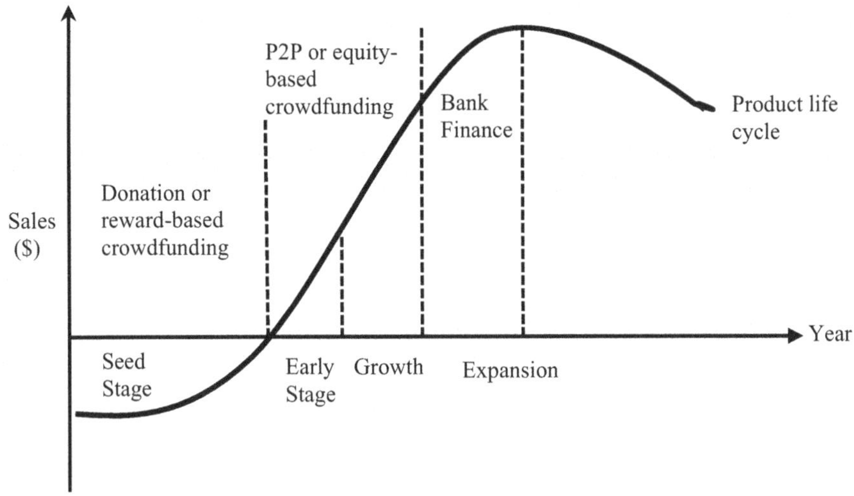

Fig. 2.2 Crowdfunding adoption curve. *Source* Authors' construction

them can separately or collectively supply finance to the startups and growth firms. Also, crowdfunding does not compete with the institutional capital such as loans from commercial banks or investment banks because the purpose of crowdfunding is to provide funding supports to the early stage (sometimes, growth stage too) of a firm that does not have sufficient assets to be placed at banks as collaterals for obtaining loans. In fact, crowdfunding aids the mainstream financing such as private equity, venture capital, and angel funds to facilitate the growth of firms to obtain institutional capital such as bank loans at a later stage. It is worth to note that developing countries do not have a sufficient number of venture capital firms and angel investors to provide finance to the growth firms although they have substantial reservoirs of entrepreneurial talent (World Bank 2013). Thus, crowdfunding has ample potential in developing countries to leapfrog the traditional financial markets to the developed economies.

2.3 Crowdfunding Models

Crowdfunding leverages the power of information technology, particularly social media and networks, to supply less cost finance to the fund seekers. Thus, crowdfunding models could be simple or complex depending on the objectives of providing returns to the fund suppliers. In general, the donation-based crowdfunding and reward-based crowdfunding take a simple form, as the fundraising platform could be set up within the entities seeking finance or may be asked an outside independent crowdfunding platform to raise funds for them without taking many legal formalities. By contrast, the financial return-based crowdfunding platforms tend to be varied and intricated in their business models. The structure of the financial return-based crowdfunding model largely depends on the level of trust, rooms for opportunism, access to information technology, the willingness of the people, the status of legal regulations, and the objectives of setting up the platforms. Taking the above issues in the account, we discuss models that are commonly used under the community-based crowdfunding and then discuss popular business models that are used by the financial return-based crowdfunding platforms.

2.3.1 Community-Based Crowdfunding Model

Under the community-based crowdfunding approach, the fund seeking organizations create a separate blog on their website or ask a crowdfunding platform to mobilize funds for them (Flowchart 2.1 and 2.2). In the former case, the fund campaigning is done by the fund seeking organizations themselves (Flowchart 2.1), whereas this is done by an independent crowdfunding platform, in the latter case, usually for a fixed fee or a percentage of the collected funds (Flowchart 2.2). In this approach, investors usually do not expect any financial return (donation-based crowdfunding) on their funds and repayment of principal as well, although they can receive a token gift in kind (reward-based crowdfunding). As a result, community-based crowdfunding is mainly used by charitable institutions or by research institutions.

Flowchart 2.1 Self-initiative crowdfunding

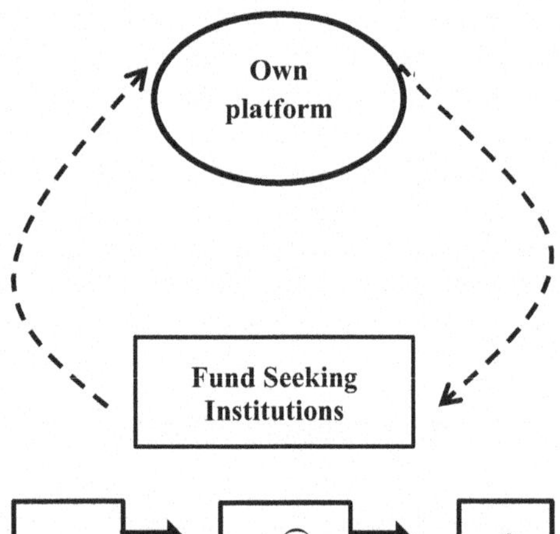

Flowchart 2.2 Independent crowdfunding. *Source* Authors' construction

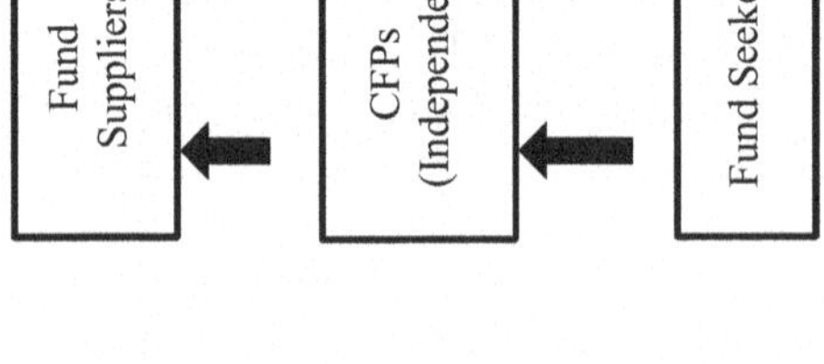

2.3.2 *Financial Return-Based Crowdfunding Model*

Financial return-based crowdfunding is used for a business motive, such as to finance the working capital requirement of a firm, to expand product lines, to purchase a sophisticated facility or anything that is important for advancing the growth of a firm. Financial return-based crowdfunding can take many forms depending on the socioeconomic dynamics of a country and characteristics of fund suppliers. Some of the popular financial return-based crowdfunding models are discussed below.

2.3.2.1 Client Segregated Model

Under this model, an individual fund supplier (debt instrument) meets with an individual borrower through the crowdfunding platforms (CFPs), and they set debt contract between them with little participation by the CFPs. CFPs offer automated bidding option that helps lenders to bid on loans in an auction style. All funds from lenders and borrowers are kept in a legally separated client account to avoid conflicts between platform's own assets and funds with lenders and borrowers in the event of bankruptcy. This practice also ensures the existence of contractual obligation between lenders and borrowers even after the platform's failure. In this arrangement, CPFs receive a loan origination fee from the borrower, either at a flat rate or a percentage of the loan amount funded. The lender pays a fixed administration fee for assessing the creditworthiness of the borrowing firm and collecting the loan repayment. The lender is also charged by additional fees if they use other services provided by the platform such as sell of loan portfolio on a secondary market. Flowchart 2.3 presents the client segregated crowdfunding model.

2.3.2.2 Notary Model

Under the notary model, CFPs introduce an individual borrower to many lenders so that the lenders can bid on the loans they want in their portfolios. The loan is originated when the amount of fund reaches the required level. However, in this case, CFPs do not originate the loan. The loan is originated by a bank. Then, CPFs issue a legal note (notary) to each lender for the value of his/her contribution to the loan. This process, in fact, shifts the risk of loan non-repayment from the loan originator (bank) to the lenders themselves. In this model, the CPFs receive a fee structure similar to that in the client segregated account model. This is a popular funding approach in the US and particularly used by the Prosper and Lending Club platform (Kirby and Worner 2014). Flowchart 2.4 summarizes this model.

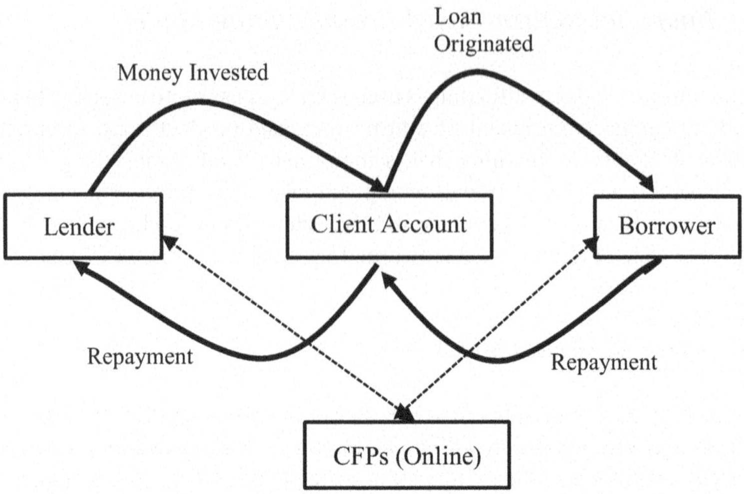

Flowchart 2.3 Client segregated model. *Source* Adapted by authors' from Kirby and Worner (2014)

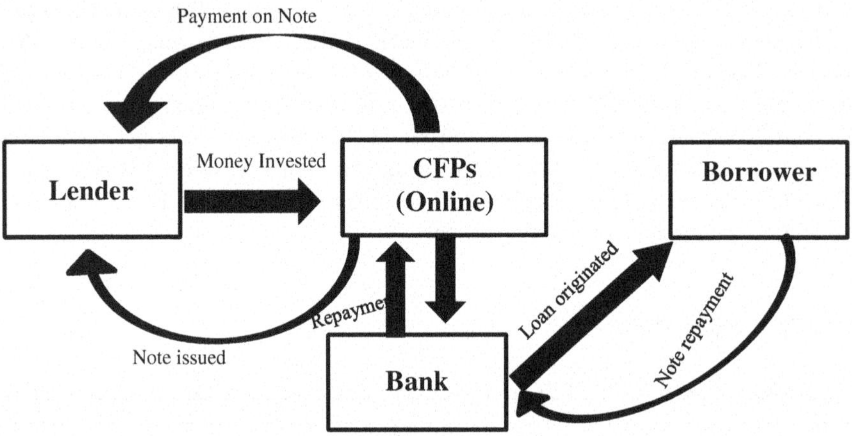

Flowchart 2.4 Notary model. *Source* Adapted by authors' from Kirby and Worner (2014)

2.3.2.3 Guaranteed Return Model

This model allows a lender to invest in a borrowing firm at a fixed rate of return guaranteed by CFPs (Flowchart 2.5). Under this approach, CFPs assume the risk of non-repayment of funds on behalf of the borrowers and provide a guaranteed return to the suppliers of funds. This model can be extended to an offline guaranteed return model or an automated guaranteed return model. In the offline guaranteed return model, investors look for potential borrowers at their local community through face to face communication and assess their creditworthiness. Then, the loan is listed on

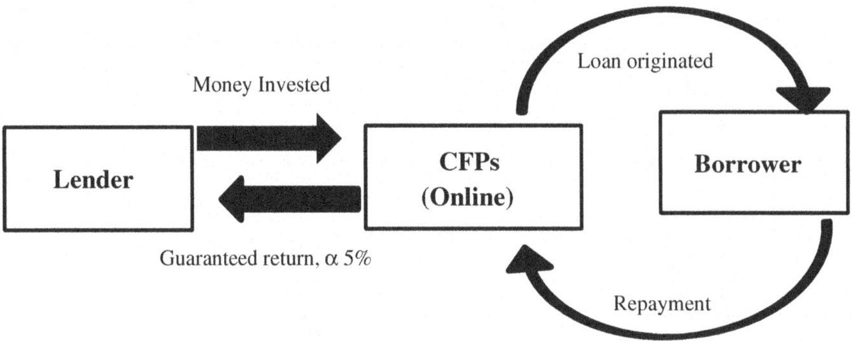

Flowchart 2.5 Guaranteed return model. *Source* Adapted by authors' from Kirby and Worner (2014)

the CFPs so that the lenders can invest in the loan. Once the loan is originated, CFPs take the responsibility to pay a fixed return to the lender over the tenure of the loan. This model is trendy in China and used by a famous crowdfunding platform, Credit Ease (Kirby and Worner 2014).

By contrast, in the automated guaranteed return model, lenders deposit their investible funds in CFPs in advance, and then, CFPs invest those funds to available borrowers through their investment preference metrics. For borrowers, the loan usually contains a 12% interest rate with a 14 days grace period. Lenders also need to pay CFPs a fixed fee for administering the loan. The lenders, in return, receive a 12% assured return from CFPs. This method is practiced by TrustBody International AB in Norway (Kirby and Worner 2014).

2.3.2.4 Equity-Based Crowdfunding Model

In this model, firms seeking external equity finance ask the CFPs to post their offerings on campaign pages. Then, they use social media and personal networks to invite investors to buy their shares. Once a share is bought, investors become equity stakeholder and receive a return on their investment either in the form of dividends or capital gains. However, investors need to take the risk of finance by themselves, as they buy an equity stake and become the residual claimants of the investee firm. On the other hand, CFPs receive a flat rate from the borrowing firms on the raised funds. CFPs also receive a fixed fee from the firms for doing the public relation activities on their behalf. This type of crowdfunding is suitable for the startups and young firms because these firms can receive a significant amount of non-contractual funds from the crowd in a short period which is essential to their growth. Crowdcube in the U.K. is a famous example of this type of platform (Kirby and Worner 2014). Notably, equity CFPs perform the similar functions that a stock exchange does. Therefore, the application of equity crowdfunding requires the compliance of the security laws

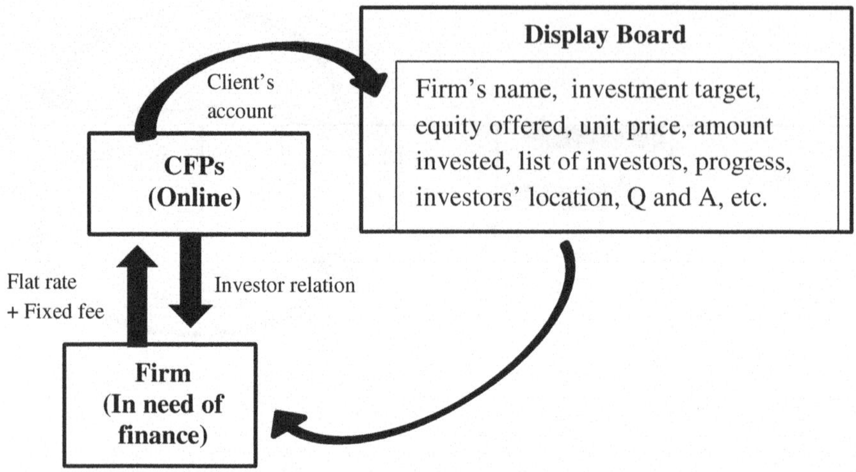

Flowchart 2.6 Equity-based crowdfunding model. *Source* Authors' construction

of a country to protect investors from frauds and unfair practices (Flowchart 2.6 summarizes the equity-based crowdfunding approach).

2.4 Crowdfunding Model—An Extension

It is worth noting that although the crowdfunding models discussed above are presently found in practice, there could be more complicated models depending on the investors' sentiment, capital market development, and financial structure of a country. One of such models could be, say, "Crowdfunding Asset Securitization Model"[1] (Flowchart 2.7). In the crowdfunding asset securitization model, the CFPs create marketable debt securities (derivative security) by pledging their loan assets to a traditional stock market. In other words, under this model, CFPs link their assets to the organized security markets by creating derivative securities offering attractive interest rates to the buyers of the security. CFPs usually create a Special Purpose Vehicle (SPV) to issue a derivative debt security, to collect the sale proceeds, and to pay the obligations (interest and principle) to the investors. SPV can also appoint professional merchant bankers to issue such derivative securities in the organized market for a fixed fee or on a percentage of commission (Flowchart 2.7). Apparently, this type of model is very complex by nature, and it requires utmost care by the security agents to prevent any unexpected financial mishaps.

[1]To our knowledge, we first point out such a model.

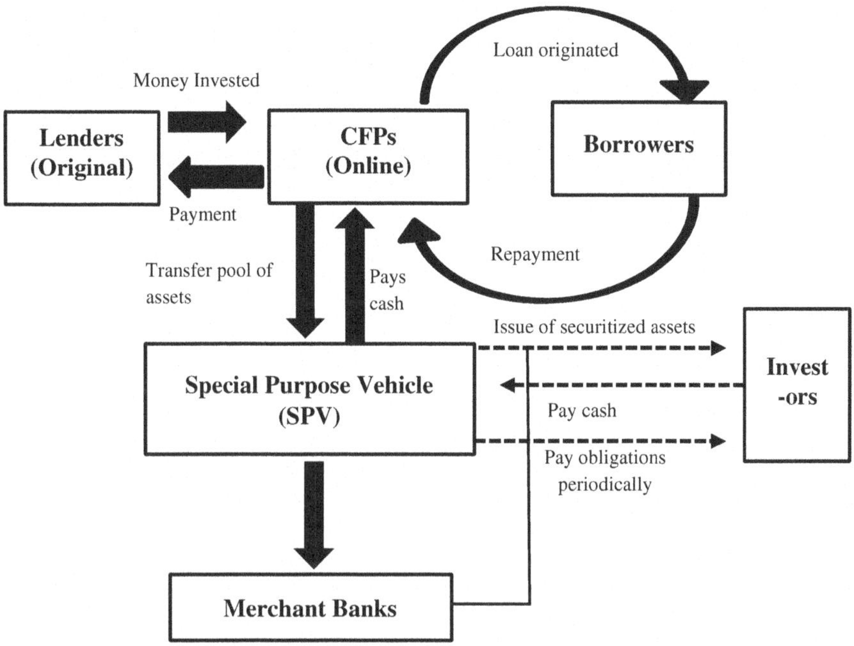

Flowchart 2.7 Crowdfunding asset securitization model. *Source* Authors' construction

2.5 Popular Crowdfunding Platforms

As previously mentioned, CFPs facilitate raising capital for the entrepreneurs through online social networks. As a facilitator of funds, CFPs usually charge a fee for their services performed for the investors' and the entrepreneurs' as well. The fees are charged to cover administrative expenses, expenses incurred for campaigns of funds, and to have some profits. Besides, crowdfunding platforms commit costs to ensure accountability and transparency in online operations and to guarantee the online security. Table 2.1 presents a list of popular crowdfunding platforms along with service fees, lending models and country of origins.

Table 2.1 List of popular crowdfunding platforms in 2016

Name	Industry focus	Model	Service charge	Setup year	Country
Kickstarter	Art, Comics, Dance, Design, Fashion, Film, Food, Games, Music, Photography, Publishing, Technology	Reward	Flat, 5% on raised capital	2009	USA
Indiegogo	Education, Technology, Film, Medicine, Medical Expense	Donation/Reward	Flexible, 4–9% based on success of goals plus 3.5% for credit card processing	2008	USA
Justgiving	Charities, Gift, Medical Illness, Sports, Natural Disasters	Donation	Flat, 5% of raised capital plus credit card processing fees		UK
GoFundMe	Medical Illness, Game, and Accidents	Reward/Donation	Flat, 5% of donated amount	2010	USA
Ulule	Unique projects in areas of art, technology, Sports, Films or humanities	Reward	Flexible, 5–6.87% based on raised capital	2010	France
Lufax	Any business products and Ideas	Peer-to-peer Lending	Flat, 4% of each fund (loan)	2011	China
Fundrazr	Medical Care, Memorials, Animal Rescue	Reward	Flat, 5% of each fund	2008	Canada
Lending Club	Personal loans, trading of loans in the secondary market and IPOs	Peer-to-peer Lending	Return on loans is 5.47–10.22%	2006	USA
Prosper	Any loan products	Peer-to-peer Lending	Average return on loans is 10.69%	2005	USA
Yooli	Loans for Chinese microfinance investors	Peer-to-peer Lending	Average return on loans is 15%	2012	China
Jimubox	SME loans and individual consumer loans for Chinese Borrowers	Peer-to-peer Lending	Borrowers: 2.5% (personal loans only) and 0.75–2% for account management From lenders: 10% of interest returns and 0.5% for service fees	2013	China

(continued)

Table 2.1 (continued)

Name	Industry focus	Model	Service charge	Setup year	Country
RateSetter	"Provision Fund"—an internal fund to ensure against borrower default, and personal loan	Peer-to-peer Lending	Average return on loans is 3.1–5% depending on amount of loans	2009	UK
Zopa	"One size fits all" strategy. Any business and personal loan	Peer-to-peer Lending	Return on loans is 6.5% for Zopa core, and 6.1% for Zopa Plus	2005	UK
CrowdCube	Equity and bonds to business	Equity/lending	Return on bond is 6.5–8.00% Equity: varies by projects 10–26%	2011	UK
Funding Circle	Any business loans	Peer-to-peer Lending	Return on loans is 6.5% for A+ grade loans	2010	UK
OurCrowd	Equity to early stage startups	Equity	–	2013	Israel
Equity Net	Equity to small business	Equity	–	2005	USA
Angelist	Technology startups that need seed funding	Equity	–	2010	USA
YouCaring	Personal, Medical, and Charitable Causes	Donation	No fees. Donation charge 2.9% of the fund plus $.30 per transaction	2011	USA
RocketHub	Music, Comics, scientists, Game, Film, Photography, Publishing, and Philanthropy	Reward	Flexible, 4–8% based on the success of campaigns plus 4% for credit card processing	2010	USA

Source Compiled by authors' from the website of individual CFP

References

Kirby E, Worner S (2014) Crowd-funding: an infant industry growing first. *IOSCO Staff Working Paper*, SWP3/2014, IOSCO, USA

Shu C (2013) Wine Retailers Nakedwins.com Savors $10 Million in New Funding. https://techcrunch.com/2013/08/22/nakedwines/

World Bank (2013) Crowdfunding potentials for the developing world. *Info Dev*, Finance and Private Sector Development Department, Washington D.C.

Chapter 3
Crowdfunding—Trends and Growth

3.1 Size and Growth of Crowdfunding Industry

As mentioned in Chap. 1, crowdfunding is a new phenomenon in market-based finance. This new form of financial technology emerged in the wake of 2008 financial meltdown in response to the increased difficulties faced by the startups and small firms in obtaining funds from the traditional banking system. So, the industry is still in an infant stage although it is snowballing.

In fact, the crowdfunding industry grew from $0.53 billion in 2009 to $34.4 billion in 2015, reflecting a 103% growth rate on an average over this period (Fig. 3.1). In 2014, the industry grew by 166% in comparison to the previous year (2013). Although the growth rate shrunk to 112% in 2015 compared to the growth rate 166% in 2014, the growth rate of the industry is still undoubtedly impressive.

Figure 3.2 portrays the size of crowdfunding industry in 2015 by regions. Figure 3.2 outlines that the crowdfunding industry is mainly concentrated on North America ($17.25bn) followed by Asia ($10.54bn), and Europe ($6.48bn). Besides, Oceania, South America, and Africa show growth in crowdfunding although the amount invested through crowdfunding in those regions lags far behind that of North America, Asia, and Europe.

As regards to the growth in crowdfunding industry against venture capital and angel finance, Fig. 3.3 outlines that the crowdfunding industry exceeds angel investment in 2015 and the trend is to exceed the venture capital finance in next couple of years. Importantly, equity crowdfunding reached to $2.5 billion in 2015 (Barnett 2015). The equity crowdfunding expects to reach $36 billion by 2020 and may surpass the venture capital industry as a significant source of startups finance (Barnett 2015).

B. K. Adhikary et al., *Crowdfunding*, SpringerBriefs in Economics,
https://doi.org/10.1007/978-981-13-1522-0_3

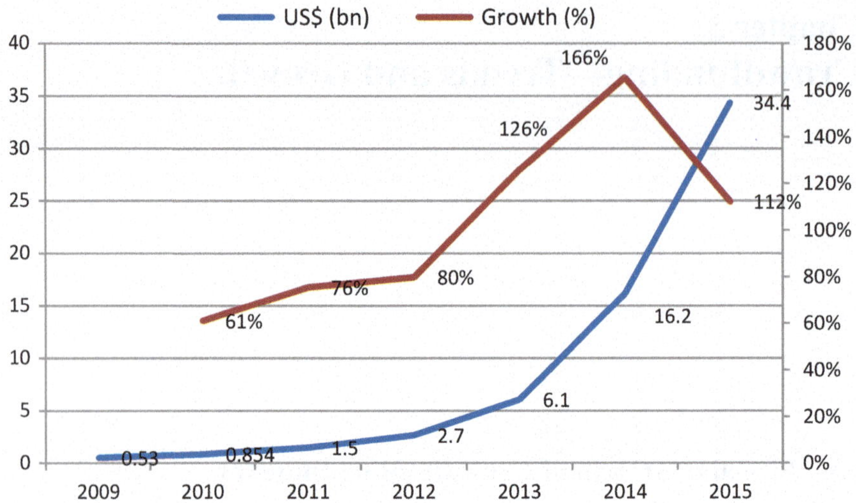

Fig. 3.1 Size and growth of crowdfunding industry. *Source* Authors' construction from 2015 CF report, Massolution.com

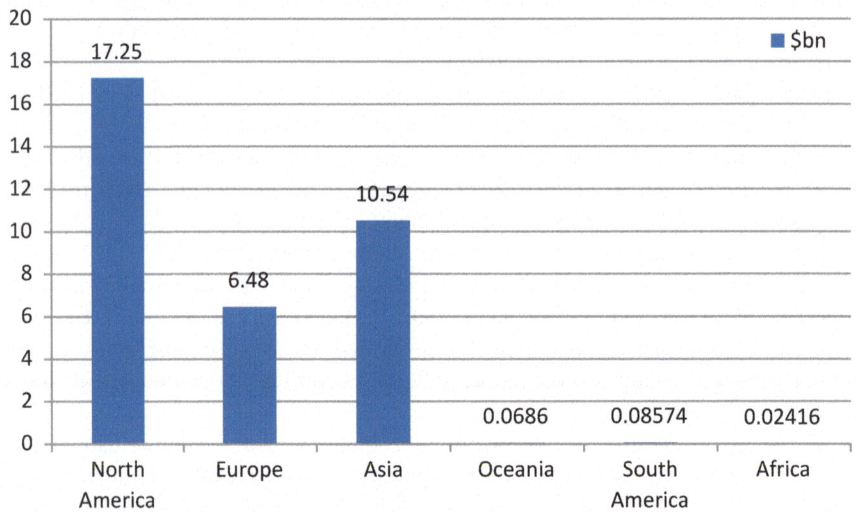

Fig. 3.2 Crowdfunding industry by regions in 2015 ($bn). *Source* Authors' construction from 2015 CF report, Massolution.com

3.2 Number and Growth of Crowdfunding Platforms

As to the number and growth in crowdfunding platforms (CFPs) worldwide, Fig. 3.4 reveals that the number of active CFPs grew from 100 in 2007 (the inception period

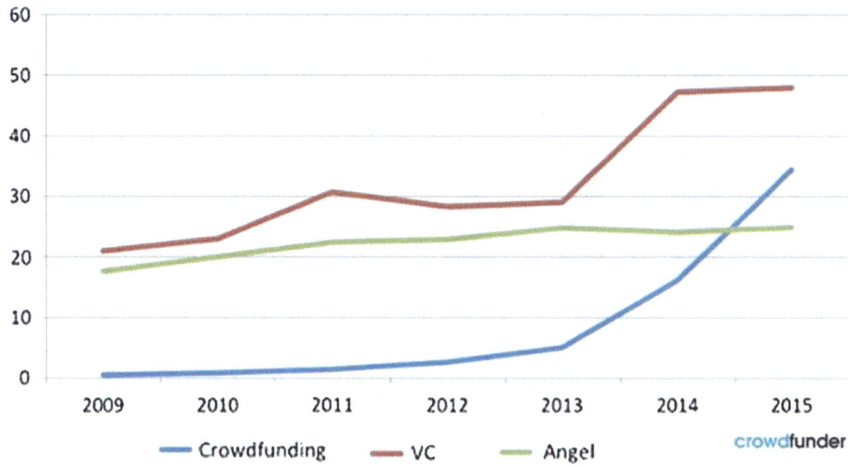

Fig. 3.3 Crowdfunding versus venture capital versus angel financing (in $bn). *Source* Adapted by authors' from Barnett (2015), Crowdfunder.com

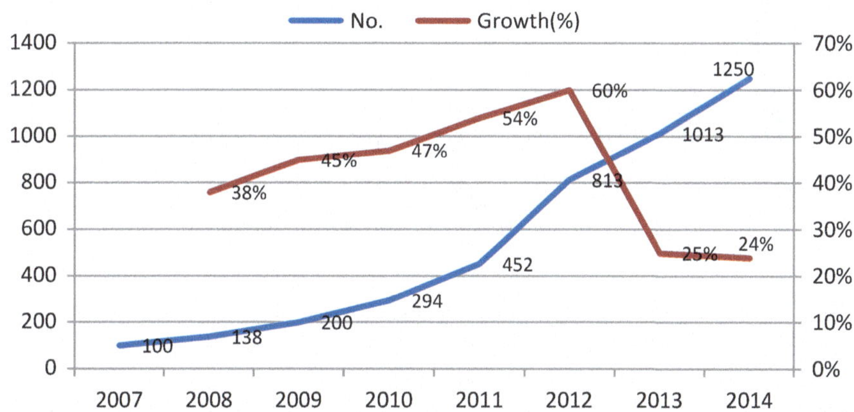

Fig. 3.4 Number and growth of crowdfunding platforms (2007–2014). *Source* Authors' construction from 2015 CF report, Massolution.com

of the industry) to 1250 in 2014, showing a 1250% growth rate in 2014 against the base year 2007. The average year to year growth rate in CFPs is nearly 39% over the period 2007–2014.

Figure 3.5 presents the number of active CFPs worldwide in 2014. As revealed by Fig. 3.5, Europe holds 600 CFPs (48% of the world CFPs) in 2014 followed by North America that captures 30% of the world CFPs. Importantly, Asia owns nearly 14% of the global CFPs, indicating an attractive place for crowdfunding in recent time. South America, Oceania, and Africa also have some CFPs for the startups financing.

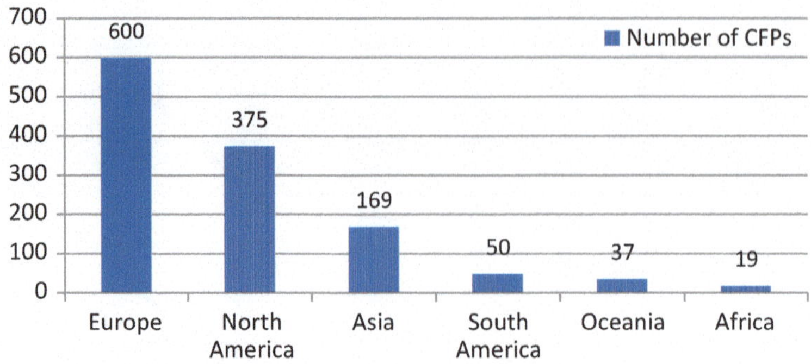

Fig. 3.5 Number of crowdfunding platforms worldwide (2014). *Source* Authors' construction from 2015 CF report, Massolution.com

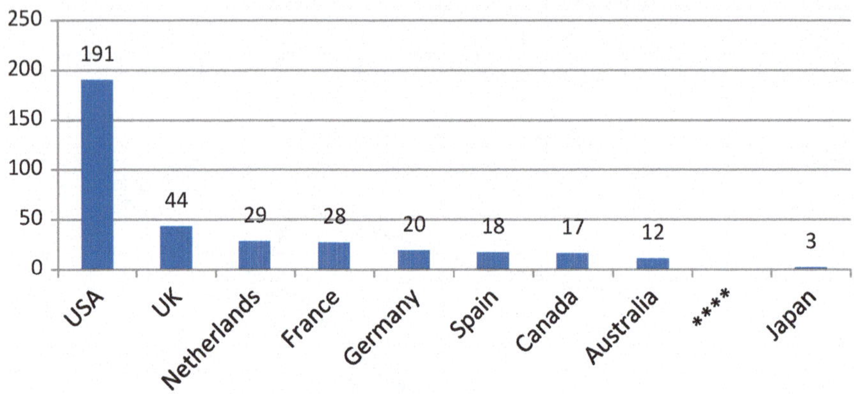

Fig. 3.6 Number of crowdfunding platforms by leading countries (2012). *Source* Authors' construction from 2015 CF report, Massolution.com

Concerning the number of CFPs by countries, Fig. 3.6 shows that the USA alone holds 191 CFPs (approximately 48% of the world CFPs) in 2012 followed by the UK and Netherlands that hold 44 and 29 CFPs, respectively. In recent time, however, China has appeared as a significant source of crowdfunding in Asia. According to Statista Report (2017a, b), China has 5500 P2P (P2P) lending platforms in 2016.

3.3 Growth of Crowdfunding by Types of Crowdfunds

Figure 3.7 exhibits the global funding volume in crowdfunding industry in 2015, by source. Importantly, among the different types of crowdfunding, the lending-based crowdfunding holds lion shares as compared to other forms (Fig. 3.7), representing the attractiveness of P2P lending.

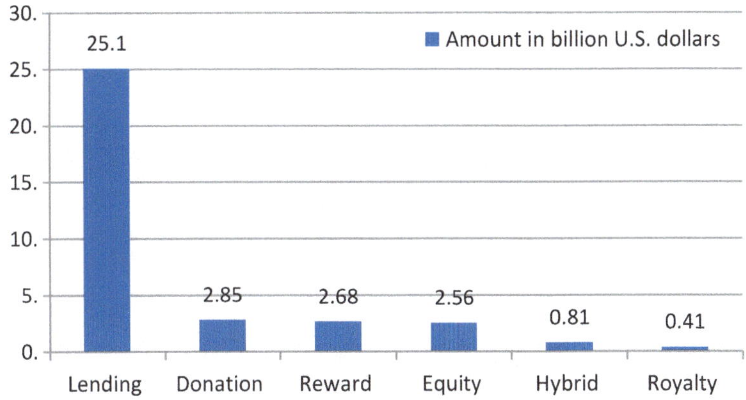

Fig. 3.7 Crowdfunding growth by types of crowdfunds (2015). *Source* Authors' construction from 2015 CF report, Massolution.com

On the other hand, the donation-based, reward-based, and equity-based crowdfunding tends to show somewhat similar performance in providing finance. However, the equity-based crowdfunding received phenomenal importance in the last couple of years due to changes in laws ("Regulation A+" and "Reg Crowdfunding" of the USA) that allowed equity crowdfunding to business houses. Besides, the hybrid and royalty-based crowdfunding popped up as other forms of crowdfunding in recent time (Fig. 3.7).

Figure 3.8 demonstrates crowdfunding investment by types of crowdfunding in the UK over the past couple of years (2014–2015). As depicted in Fig. 3.8, the P2P business lending captures the largest volume in crowdfunding (£1490 million) in 2015 followed by the P2P consumer lending (£909 million). By contrast, the equity-based crowdfunding bags £332 million in 2015 as against £84 million in 2014, suggesting that the equity-based crowdfunding has been the second-best option for crowdfunding in the UK. On the other hand, the donation-based crowdfunding market contributed to £12 million in funding value in 2015.

Figure 3.9 portrays crowdfunding transactions by types of crowdfunding in Europe (excluding the UK) in a million € in 2015. Figure 3.9 indicates that the equity-based crowdfunding reached a total transaction value of €159 million in 2015 following the reward-based crowdfunding (€139 million). In fact, the equity-based crowdfunding grew from €18.4 million in 2012 to €159 million, a 764% growth rate over the span of 4 years (2012–2015), implying that the equity-based crowdfunding has been the most popular way to obtain finance in European countries than the UK.

Notably, Europe tends to have a growing number of P2P consumer and P2P business lending transactions in some recent years. For instance, the value of P2P consumer lending increased to €366 million in Europe (excluding the UK) in 2015 from €62.5 million in 2012. Similarly, the value of P2P business lending grew from

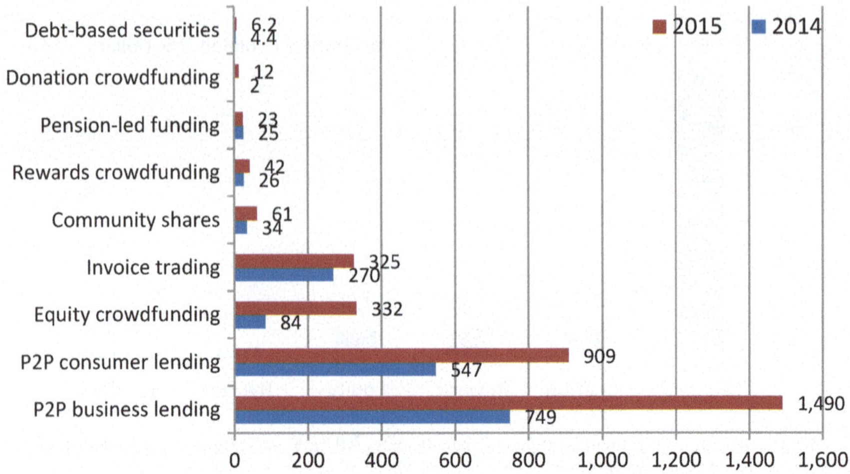

Fig. 3.8 Crowdfunding in the UK by types of crowdfunds in £ million (2014–2015). *Source* Authors' construction from Statistia.com (2017a, b)

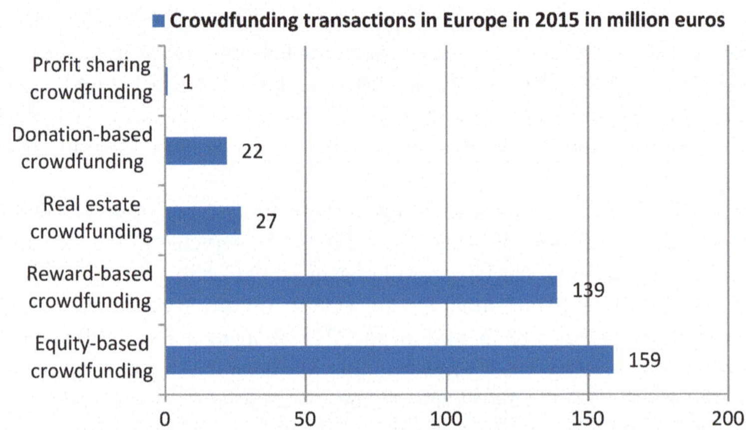

Fig. 3.9 Crowdfunding in Europe (except the UK) by types of crowdfunds. *Source* Authors' construction from Statistia.com (2017a, b)

a tiny amount of €7.8 million in 2012 to €212 million in 2015, a 2617% growth rate in 2015 when compared with the base year 2012 (Fig. 3.10).

Precisely, European investors mostly prefer P2P business and P2P consumer lending followed by the equity-based crowdfunding to provide finance to the entrepreneurs. Besides, reward-based crowdfunding continues to be a favorite source of funds for small businesses and philanthropic organizations. Moreover, real estate crowdfunding platforms have popped up in recent time to enable investors to invest in the real estate sector.

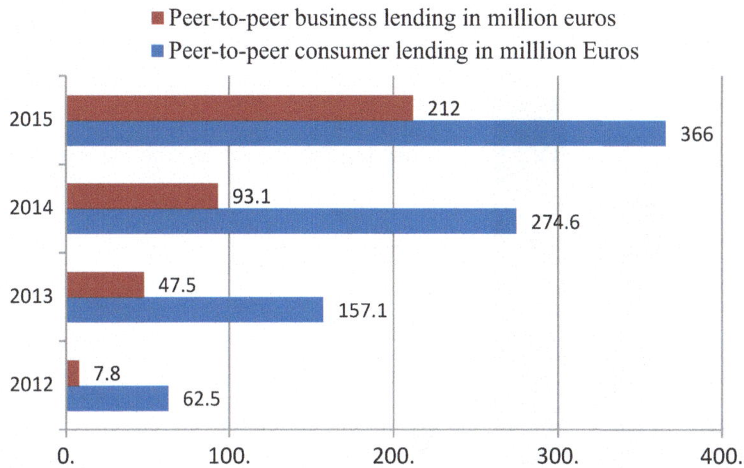

Fig. 3.10 P2P business and consumer lending in Europe (except the UK) from 2012 to 2015 (in a million €). *Source* Authors' construction from Statistia.com

On the other hand, the online alternative finance market (crowdfunding) within the Americas reached to $35.2bn in 2016 from $11.7 bn in 2014 and $28.7bn in 2015 (Fig. 3.11). The Americas alternative finance market grew by 23% in 2016 compared to the previous year (2015). Importantly, within the Americas, the USA alone accounts for 98% of the online alternative finance market and the rest 2% are shared by Canada and Latin America. The alternative finance industry in the USA grew by 22% in 2016 as against the year 2015.

As regards to the investment by alternative finance models across Americas, Fig. 3.12 reports that the P2P Consumer Lending has been the most popular approach to financing, but it experienced a considerable annual growth rate decline in 2016 (17%), especially when compared to the triple-digit yearly growth of 2015 (135%). In 2016, this model accounted for $21.1bn of the total Americas alternative finance volume. Besides, the Balance Sheet Business Lending appeared as the second highest volume-generating model in the region, with $6.1 billion in 2016, surpassing other forms of business financing region-wide. All other models, however, grew modestly or declined slightly over this period (2014–2016).

Concerning the growth of crowdfunding in the Asian region, China has based emerged as a leading country followed by Indonesia, Singapore, Malaysia, Thailand, and Japan. According to the Statistia.com (2017a, b), the transaction volume in crowdfunding industry in the Asian region reached to $5.6bn in 2017, almost 98% of this investment was made in China. Figure 3.13 provides the growth of P2P transaction amounts and number of P2P platforms in China over the period 2012–2016. Figure 3.13 illustrates that the number of P2P platforms in China increased from 200 in 2012 to 3443 in 2015 although it showed a declining trend in 2016 (2448). This decline is, however, endorsed to the regulation on P2P lending that came into effect

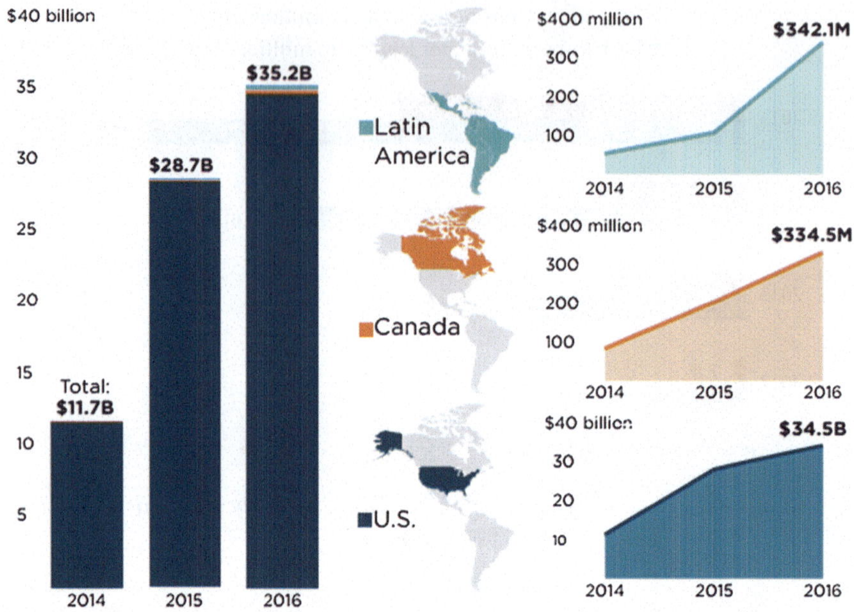

Fig. 3.11 Alternative finance market in Americas, 2014–2016. *Source* Adapted by authors' from Ziegler et al. (2017), the report on Americas Alternative Finance Industry, 2017

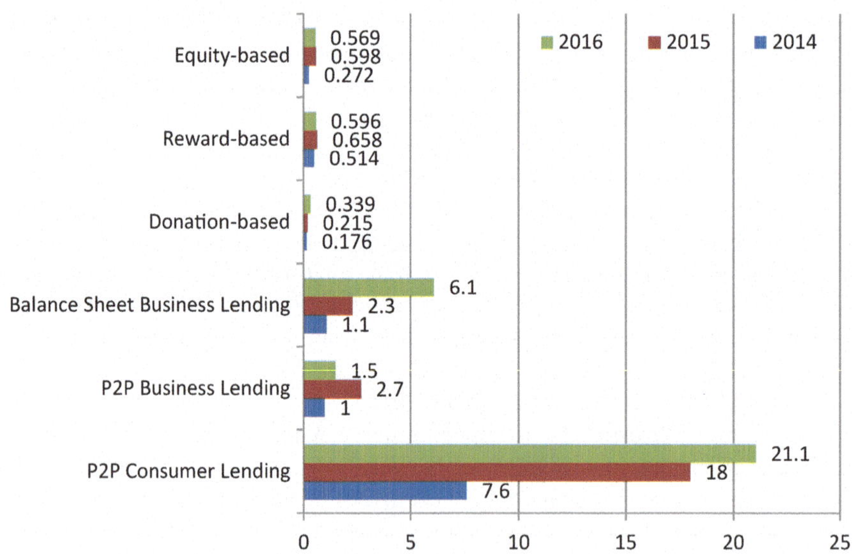

Fig. 3.12 Alternative finance market in Americas by models, 2014–2016. *Source* Adapted by authors' from the report on Americas Alternative Finance Industry, 2017

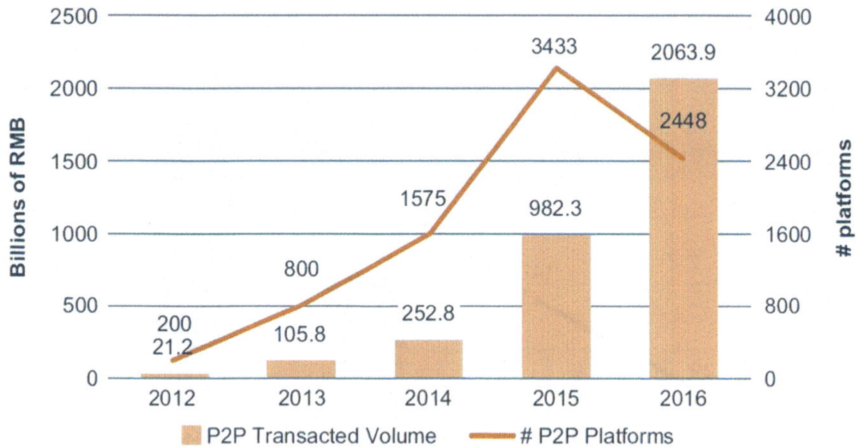

Fig. 3.13 P2P transaction volume and number of platforms in China, 2012–2016. *Source* Adapted by authors' from Aveni and Jenik (2017)

in 2015. Notably, the transaction amounts in P2P lending continued to grow from ¥21.2bn in 2012 to ¥2063.9bn in 2016. The industry increased by nearly 111% as compared to the last year (2015).

Figure 3.14 shows the growth of crowdfunding in China by models over the period 2012–2016. Figure 3.14 reveals that the reward-based crowdfunding is most popular in China as against the donation-based crowdfunding. For instance, while the donation-based crowdfunding declined to ¥0.45bn in 2016 from ¥0.63bn in 2015, the reward-based crowdfunding grew by 198% from ¥5.60bn in 2015 to ¥16.73bn in 2016. One of the reasons for the fall of donation-based crowdfunding is that Chinese people usually discourage philanthropic activities. By contrast, reward-based platforms are closely intertwined with e-commerce through major Chinese technology companies, particularly Alibaba, Tencent, and Jing Dong, which build multi-functional platforms for e-commerce and online retail services. Thus, reward-based crowdfunding tends to capture significant shares of crowdfunding in China. On the other hand, the equity-based crowdfunding is relatively new in China. Equity-based crowdfunding accounts for ¥5.30bn in 2016 while it was ¥5.19bn in 2015. Recently, the Chinese government has continued to support equity crowdfunding outwardly, so, higher growth in equity crowdfunding is likely to return in the next couple of years.

With respect to the growth of Chinese P2P market, Morgan Stanley (2015) provides a comparative picture of P2P lending among four leading countries such as China, the USA, the UK and Australia in its research blue paper, "Global Marketplace Lending: Disruptive Innovation in Financials." According to the report, Chinese P2P lending will reach $147.7bn in 2019, followed by the USA ($98.2bn), and the UK ($18.3bn). In 2020, the Chinese P2P market expects to show a decline but still, it

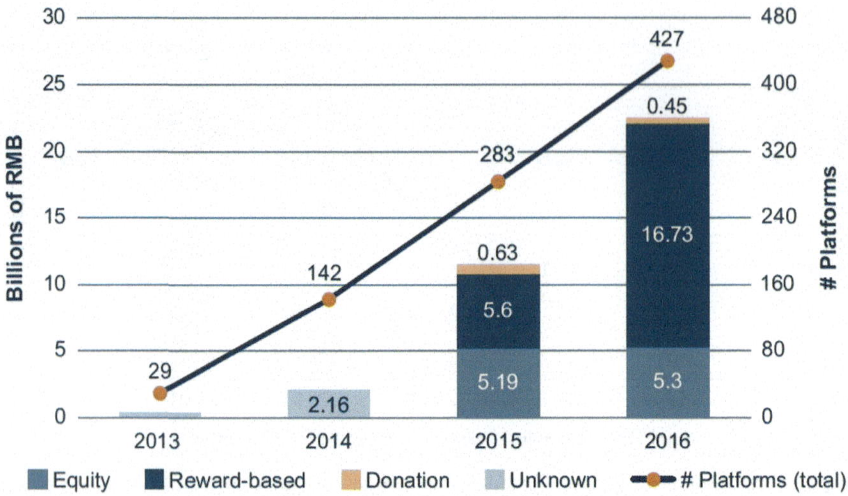

Fig. 3.14 Crowdfunding in China by models (P2P excluded), 2012–2016. *Source* Adapted by authors' from Aveni and Jenik (2017)

will dominate the world's P2P market, and the projected cumulative average growth would be 51% over the period 2015–2020 (Fig. 3.15).

3.4 Crowdfund Investment by Sectors

Regarding the sectors for crowdfunding investment, the three areas, namely technology, design, and gaming are found to be the most popular sectors globally. Figure 3.16 shows that technology sector received $229.96 million in 2016 followed by design and gaming sectors that bagged $176.09 million and $106.28 million, respectively in 2016. The other attractive sectors for crowdfunding investment are film, fashion, music, publishing, video games, food, and art industries.

Figure 3.17 portrays attractive sectors for crowdfunding investment in the USA in 2016. Akin to world's trend, the technology, design, and gaming sectors are found to be the most attractive sectors for investment in the USA in 2016. The technology sector captured $150.80 million in 2016 followed by design and gaming sectors that took $115.66 million and $77.99 million, respectively in 2016.

By contrast, in the UK, the most attractive sector for crowdfunding investment has been the gaming sector followed by design, technology, and community sectors. Figure 3.18 depicts that total amount of money raised via crowdfunding in the gaming sector amounted to approximately $12.42 million in 2016. In the same year, the design, technology, and community sectors captured $10.52, 9.07, and 6.93 million, respectively. On the other hand, sectors such as music, fashion, video games, and publishing are shown to have least favorite areas for crowdfunding in the UK.

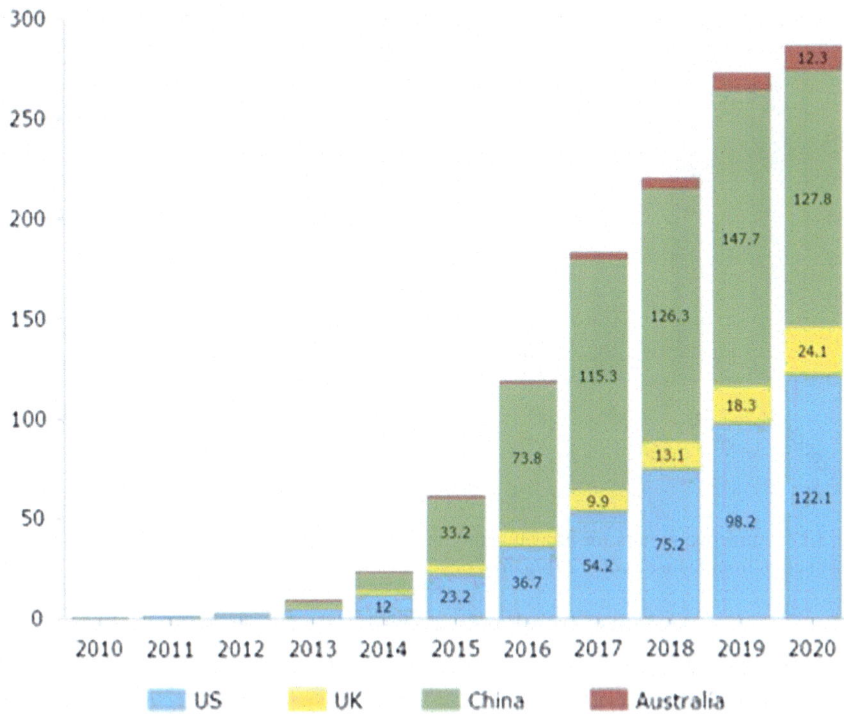

Fig. 3.15 P2P lending volume ($bn) in major economies (2010–2020). *Source* Adapted by authors' from Morgan Stanley (2015)

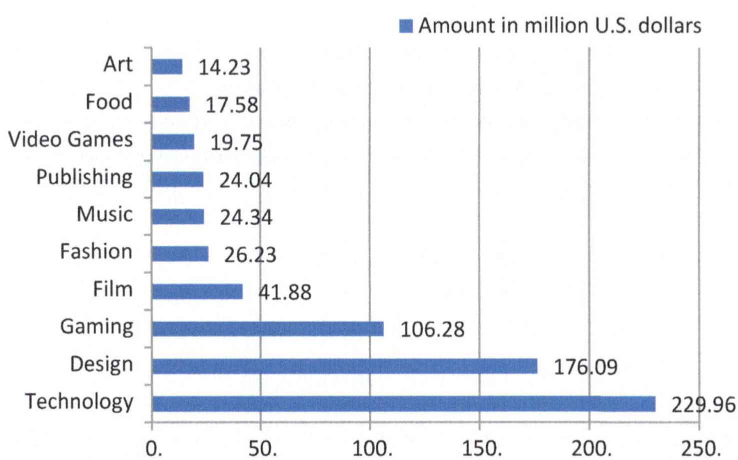

Fig. 3.16 Amount of money raised by crowdfunding globally, by sector (in 2016). *Source* Authors' construction from Statistia.com (2017a, b)

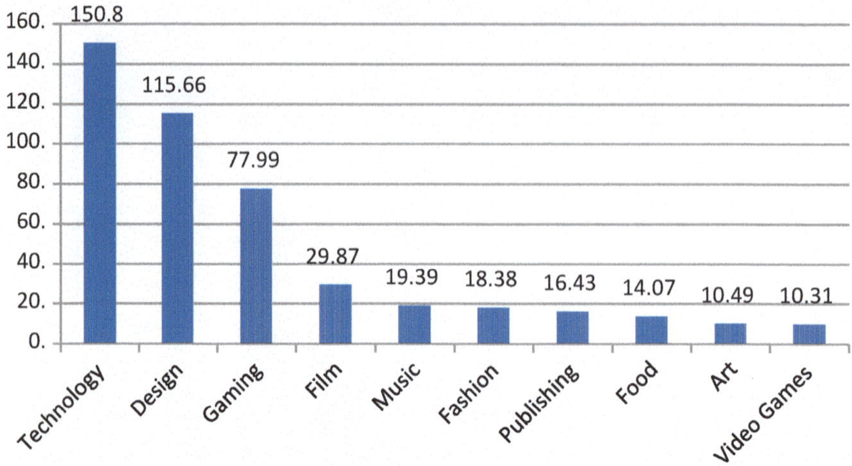

Fig. 3.17 Attractive sectors for crowdfunding in the US, by sector (in 2016). *Source* Authors' construction from Statistia.com (2017a, b)

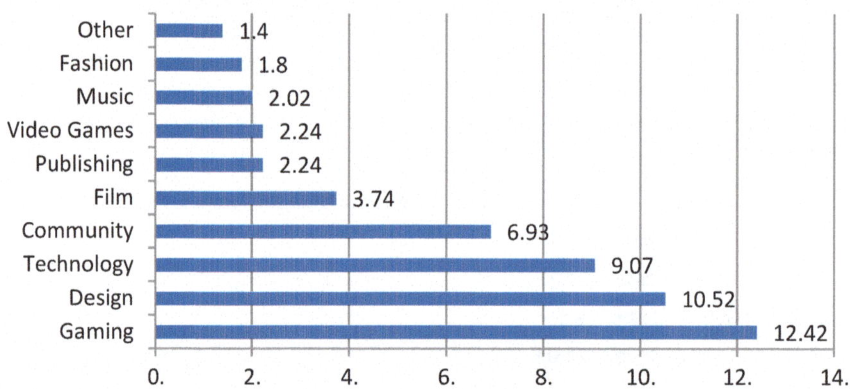

Fig. 3.18 Attractive sectors for crowdfunding in the UK, by sector (in 2016). *Source* Authors' construction from Statistia.com (2017a, b)

However, concerning the number of completed crowdfund campaigns by sectors (worldwide), Fig. 3.19, delivers that the film sector has received the highest number of campaigns (15,762) followed by technology (14,257), music (11,014), and design (8562) sectors. By contrast, the food sector requires lowest crowdfund campaigns in raising funds from the crowdfunding platforms.

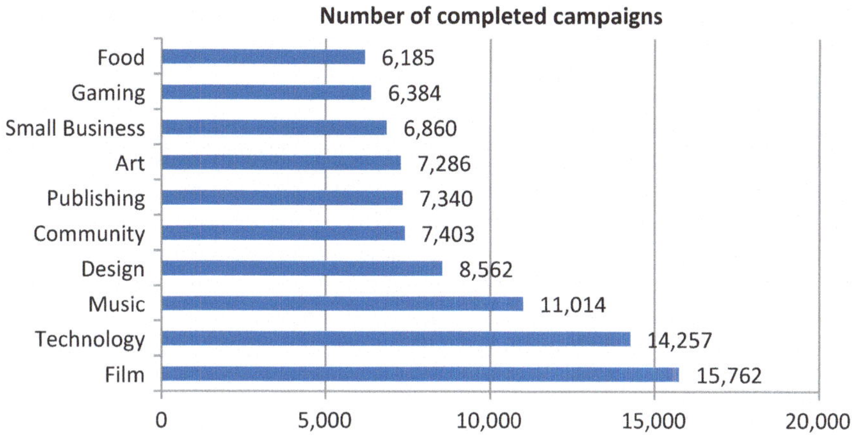

Fig. 3.19 Worldwide number of completed crowdfund campaigns, by sector (in 2016). *Source* Authors' construction from Statistia.com (2017a, b)

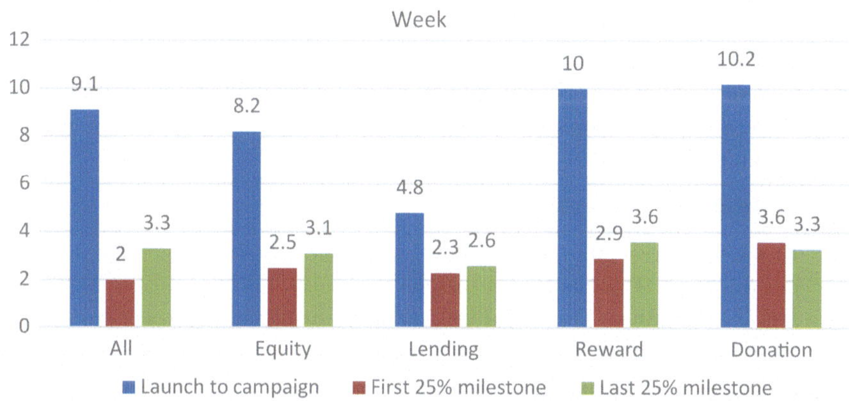

Fig. 3.20 Campaign time for types of crowdfunding. *Source* Adapted by authors' from Massolution.com (2013)

3.5 Campaign Time by Types of Crowdfunding

Regarding the time taken by the CFPs, lending-based CFPs are found to obtain finance within 4.8 weeks on an average from the date of the campaign which is, in fact, half of the time taken for projects posted in equity-based CFPs (Fig. 3.20). However, projects posted on donation-based and reward-based CFPs take about ten weeks on an average. Surprisingly, reaching the first 25% milestone and the last 25% milestone takes the almost similar amount of time (10 weeks) for all types of CFPs. As a whole, CFPs seem to be very useful in raising funds from investors in a short period, which is indeed an indicator of the future growth potential of the industry.

3.6 Risks in Crowdfunding

Although the crowdfunding is playing a more and more critical role in solving the financing problems for startups, we cannot ignore the risks and problems of crowdfunding. In recent years, hackers have demonstrated an alarming ability to break into seemingly secure data repositories of leading retailers and companies and steal credit card details and other valuable client information. A similar risk exists for crowdfunding portals and platforms, which are vulnerable to attacks from hackers and cyber-criminals. The prospect of possible credit card or identity theft from a crowdfunding portal is a risk that needs to be taken into consideration. We discuss below some issues along with their possible solutions related to risks in crowdfunding.

Issue #1. Valuation

- ✓ **Problem**: Entrepreneur usually determines the value of the business listed on a crowdfunding platform. However, this may not be an accurate representation because startups are usually not as much worth as the entrepreneur thinks. This means that investors may not get the promised return in the absence of a correct valuation.
- ✓ **Possible Solution**: This problem can be reduced by incorporating experienced lead investors such as business angels who can efficiently determine the firm's value, and by allowing sophisticated crowd investors who can perform ex-ante monitoring.

Issue #2. Inadequate Due Diligence

- ✓ **Problem**: In crowdfunding, there is inadequate time for proper and detailed due diligence. This can lead to losses.
- ✓ **Possible Solution**: This could be averted by involving an expert investment banker or an experienced angel investor who will act as a lead investor.

Issue #3. Lack of Accountability

- ✓ **Problem**: In crowdfunding, there is no accountability on the part of the startups to ensure that the money is spent wisely or as planned.
- ✓ **Possible Solution**: A way to overcome this problem would be to ask entrepreneurs to provide financial statements regularly as proof of financial progress.

Issue #4. Potential Lack of Financial Matter

- ✓ **Problem**: Equity crowdfunding potentially lacks financial matter. Unlike crowdfunding, investors can choose one to take a seat on the board of the startups in equity financing that enables him to monitor firm's financial decision on behalf of other investors.
- ✓ **Possible Solution**: Akin to traditional equity financing, in equity crowdfunding, the lead investors may demand a seat on the board of the startups to check and control financial matter.

Issue #5. Corporate Governance

✓ **Problem:** Corporate governance mechanism is missing in crowdfunding and is at the discretion of the entrepreneur.

✓ **Possible Solution**: Resembling a traditional financing situation, investors can demand that fundraisers should have a corporate governance mechanism in place. This would help investors to ensure that management is keen to advance the growth of the company.

Issue #6. Lack of Structured Communication Channels

✓ **Problem**: This is an issue that is slowly being addressed by crowdfunding websites.

✓ **Possible Solution**: As communication continues even after a campaign closes, it is essential for an entrepreneur to keep an open channel of communication with investors. An open channel may ensure that stakeholders are there to support through difficult times rather than blaming the team.

Issue #7. Lack of Entrepreneurship Guidance

✓ **Problem**: Crowdfunding lacks entrepreneurship guidance as compared to a typical financing style. The traditional venture capitalists have experience of promoting and managing a business or have broader industry contracts or observation experience. However, the investors of crowdfunding cannot provide such services. Besides, the entrepreneur may be good at researching and developing, but may not be good at marketing and packaging. Moreover, the follow-up financing, as is done by venture capitalists, becomes difficult for the crowdfund supporters, as they are likely to turn their attention to other startups.

✓ **Possible Solution**: Crowdfunding platforms (CFPs) may provide advisory services to startups for marketing and managing campaigns. CFPs may prepare a list of experienced investors, especially venture capitalists and angel investors, who can provide managerial and marketing supports before launching the final campaign for a fee. Similarly, there could be a link between venture capitalist and startups so that they can participate in growth stage financing for the startups. Simultaneously, entrepreneurs who are in growth stage may seek debt and equity finance by posting their previous year's successful performance on the crowdfunding websites.

Issue #8. Regulatory Risks

✓ **Problem:** Startups may disclose fraudulent information to raise funds. A large number of crowdfunding platforms also do not have perfect supervision system. The purpose of crowdfunding is to make more people to get involved in the projects or startups, but as a mode of investing, it may be misused when there is no regulation or have ambiguous regulations.

✓ **Possible Solution**: There should be a proper and concrete admittance criterion and quit mechanism for the startups and the crowdfunding platforms as well. An independent regulatory body could be set up to regulate crowdfunding industry.

3.7 New Directions of Crowdfunding

(a) ***Retail crowdfunding***

Although equity crowdfunding is the latest phenomenon for providing finance to startups, the retail crowdfunding is likely to be a favorite approach to financing an individual creative project in the next couple of years. The launch of Crowdemand in 2014, a retail crowdfunding platform, brought opportunities for the fashion designers and manufacturers to secure private funding to bring a design to market. Crowdemand offers exclusive designs for pre-order at a 50% deposit upfront. Once the designs are completed, customers pay the remainder. This allows fashion designers to test the popularity of their designs, secure funding for their completion and pre-sell them to an audience. Noted designer Cynthia Rowley is one of the retail platforms supporters and uses it to debut and sell her exclusive creations.

(b) ***Corporate crowdfunding***

Now, corporations are leveraging crowdfunding for their prototypes, research, and necessary finance. Recently, Indiegogo has linked its crowdfunding platform to corporates to help crowdfund their research ideas, while enticing customers to fund their favorites. This could usher in an era of corporate market research being done through public validation, support, and pre-orders before hitting the mainstream. Currently, Indiegogo's new crowdfunding program is only open to Fortune 1000 and Global 500 companies with fees that would be prohibitive to smaller firms.

(c) ***Real estate crowdfunding***

In the past, the sources of funds for the commercial real estate industry were either bank loans or equities. In some countries, investors with millions of dollars could only avail of this opportunity. Today, however, real estate crowdfunding is dismantling the old concept by inviting mass people with a smaller unit of funds for investment. For instance, RealtyMogul.com makes it possible to crowdfund a real estate property for as little as $5000. Investors can also use the platform to browse for debt or equity investments, invest online and track their performance from a centralized dashboard.

(d) ***Crowdfunding insurance***

In May 2016, American International Group (AIG) announced the launch of crowd-funded insurance to help protect equity crowdfunding platforms. Presently, AIG only covers platforms that have appropriate checks and balances in place. Its first policy-holder is Eureeca, which is poised to offer insurance protection to all investors using its portal. If AIG is successful, more crowdfunding insurance players will enter the market, starting with large-scale equity fundraising projects. Over time, more policies will trickle into small platforms, perhaps offering the kinds of a la carte services that enable sellers to choose the coverage that makes the most sense for smaller investors.

(e) ***Crowdfunding for SMEs***

Crowdfunding is likely to be a viable alternative option to finance small and medium enterprises (SMEs) in developing economies, especially for the rural financial market where non-government organizations (NGOs) mainly cater to the financing needs of the small firms in the form of microfinance. In the future, crowdfunding platforms are likely to create a link with NGOs to promote large-scale finance to the microcredit-backed firms that need growth stage financing.

References

Aveni T, Jenik L (2017) Crowdfunding in China: the financial inclusion dimension. CGAP, Washington, pp 1–4

Barnett C (2015) Trends show crowdfunding to surpass VC In 2016. http://www.forbes.com/sites/chancebarnett/2015/06/09/trends-show-crowdfunding-to-surpass-vc-in-2016/3/

Massolution.com (2013, 2015) Crowdfunding industry report, 2013, 2015

Morgan Stanley (2015) Global marketplace lending: disruptive innovation in financials. Research Blue Paper, 2015. http://www.morganstanley.com/ideas/p2p-marketplace-lending

Statistia (2017a) Number of online P2P lending platforms in China from 2010 to 2016. https://www.statista.com/statistics/652720/china-online-p2p-lending-platform-count/

Statistia (2017b) Crowdfunding volume world wide. https://www.statista.com/statistics/620952/total-crowdfunding-volume-worldwide/

Ziegler T, Reedy EJ, Lee A, Zhang B, Kroszner RS, Garvey K (2017) The 2017 Americas alternative finance industry report. Cambridge Centre for Alternative Finance. https://www.jbs.cam.ac.uk/fileadmin/user_upload/research/centres/alternative-finance/downloads/2017-05-americas-alternative-finance-industry-report.pdf

Chapter 4
Crowdfunding—Theories and Empirical Works

4.1 Theories of Crowdfunding

Crowdfunding is a web-based financial approach that falls under the ambit of new entrepreneurial finance. It leverages social media and information technology to cater to the funding needs of the startups and firms that fail to obtain finance from the commercial banks due to insufficient collateral, or they do not match with banks' lending strategies. The development of Web 2.0 has been instrumental in the development, diffusion, and growth of crowdfunding across countries. In this section, we discussed several economic theories as a foundation of crowdfunding and its rapid dissemination as well.

(i) *Social networking theory*

Social network theory puts emphasis on the strength of social structures, social relationships and group ties in understanding human behavior and flow of transactions. The concept stemmed from social psychology and sociology and became ubiquitous in the social and behavioral sciences by the 1980s (Wellman 1988; Wasserman and Faust 1994; Freeman 2004). The birth of Internet technology and the development of Web 2.0 provided additional impetus to the use of social networks to flow social capital (financial and cultural capital that flow by reciprocity, trust, and cooperation) in society. Podolny and Baron (1997) studied how informal connection between executives, employees, and associations increase the value of an organization. Valenzuela et al. (2009) traced a positive relationship between social capital and the intensity of social network while Wei et al. (2016) investigated how the removal of suspended users can impact twitter-based network structure. Since social structures and social networks influence the movement of social capital and affect economic outcomes such as hiring, pricing, productivity, and innovation (Granovetter 2005), they can be considered as an essential footing for the evolution and diffusion of crowdfunding technology.

B. K. Adhikary et al., *Crowdfunding*, SpringerBriefs in Economics,
https://doi.org/10.1007/978-981-13-1522-0_4

(ii) *Signaling theory*

The root of the signaling theory is the information asymmetry theory (Akerlof 1970) that highlights that the degree of hidden information between parties involved in a financial transaction results in disequilibrium. When one side holds superior information over others, the markets tend to reach a disequilibrium point, resulting in disappearing of the financial transaction at the extreme case. To reduce the information asymmetry problem, Spence (1973) proposed signaling theory that states that if one party gives some piece of relevant information to the other parties, it serves as a signal to commit financial transactions by offering a higher price usually than he does if he has not received the signal. Then, Leland and Pyle (1977) analyzed the role of signals in improving the success of IPOs. Further, Waldfogel and Chen (2006) demonstrated the importance of signaling in online marketplaces to create brands. Now, signaling theory is a widely used tool in mainstream finance for improving shareholders' returns and preventing unexpected fall in share prices. Since crowdfunding is a web-based financial tool for entrepreneurial firms, the quality of signaling tends to determine the success of funds. The quality of signals also banks on time, energy, or money that the senders (in this case entrepreneurs and crowdfunding platforms) like to spend on giving signals (available information), and the success of funds largely depends on how these signals are read and trusted by the investors. Thus, signaling theory serves as an important root in explaining the evolution and diffusion of crowdfunding technology.

(iii) *Theory of institutions*

North (1990) popularized the theory of 'institutions' in explaining the flow of financial transactions in international trade. The basic premise of the institutional theory is that institutional efficiencies limit opportunism and create rooms for financial innovation, thereby increasing incentives for investment (North 1990). In other words, a well-defined institutional framework promotes capital flow by reducing the transaction costs of investment. In this theory, institutions refer to the legal, economic, and political organs that serve as a lubricant for investment and growth. It also includes informal norms of behavior such as traditions, habits, and customs that influence the perception and willingness of investors in providing capital. North (1990) argues that both the formal and informal institutions create necessary incentive structures for investment and the changes in institutional settings describe the pattern of development of a country. Notably, crowdfunding is mainly an Internet-based financial tool that came out due to the weaknesses of commercial banks to cater to the financing needs of the startups. Therefore, the growth of crowdfunding can be studied from the institutional point of view to understand how institutional structures help crowdfunding platforms to mobilize social capital and ensure sound governance on the use of crowdfunds.

(iv) *Stakeholder theory*

Stakeholder theory postulates that modern corporation is a nexus of contracts among different groups of people (stakeholders) directly or indirectly affected by firm's operation (Freeman 1994). Stakeholder theory rests its foundation on several other economic theories such as agency, moral hazard, and incentives. While agency theory (Jensen and Meckling 1976) states that agency problem arises due to the separation of ownership and management, the stakeholder theory argues that the stockholders do not own assets of a corporation, but the corporation itself, and managers are accountable to the corporation, not to the stockholders. This is because stockholders sell shares when they need finance, but the corporation exists years after years, so does its customers and suppliers. This line of thinking, in fact, leads corporation to follow the policy of "caveat venditor," not "caveat emptor." Al these imply that executives should not solely focus on enhancing stockholders return instead they should provide value to the interest of other groups of people such as customers, suppliers, employees, and local community who contributes to the existence and growth of firms as well. The crowdfunding instruments facilitate the flow of social capital through viral networks where crowdfunding platforms and fundraiser are much accountable to the fund suppliers and the community as well. For instance, if owners manage the firms in the long run by taking P2P crowdfunding, the agency problem tends to be fierce. Likewise, if equity crowdfunding is obtained and the interest of shareholders is neglected at the post-fund stage, the equity crowdfunding instrument could end up with a charity one. This would also breach the trust of the community and mobilization of social capital in the future. On the above context, the stockholder theory could be instrumental in explaining the future growth and patterns of crowdfunding industry and its sustainability as well.

(v) *Theory of disruptive innovation*

Disruptive innovation refers to an instrument, process or method that significantly alters the way an organization works or market functions. Christensen coined this idea in 1997 in his book "The innovator's dilemma: when new technologies cause great firms to fail." He argues that disruption innovation (such as Facebook) is the use of disruptive technology (such as the Internet) to lead innovation-driven growth. One of the premises of the disruptive innovation theory is that it is "inherently positive." Crowdfunding is a disruptive innovation in entrepreneurial finance because it advocates an alternative way to provide finance to the startups, small firms, and technology entrepreneurs. However, the assumption of inherently positive may turn sour, especially for financial industry. One example is the Great Financial Crisis-2008 that is viewed as the resultant effects of excessive innovations in the financial industry. As crowdfunding is a new financial innovation, the instrument may generate "lemon syndrome" if fund seekers exaggerate business information and remain untouched because of regulatory loopholes. It may also bring suboptimal allocation and use of financial and social capital if investors become free riders. Therefore, the theory of disruptive innovation tends to explain the shape of the crowdfunding industry in the future.

4.2 Extant Literature of Crowdfunding

The purpose of this chapter is to provide an overview of the academic research on crowdfunding. Crowdfunding has emerged as an alternative source of finance since 2008. Thus, the academic literature of crowdfunding is still limited but growing very quickly. This review is structured according to the key players in crowdfunding: capital seekers, capital providers, and intermediaries. The review also puts some avenues for future research.

4.2.1 Crowdfunding Literature on Fund Seekers

This part is discussed according to the legal restrictions of equity-based crowdfunding, the motivations for crowdfunding, and the determinants of success.

(i) *Legal framework*

In 2009, the US scholars questioned equity crowdfunding about its legality under the purview of the Securities Act 1933 (Kappel 2009). The substantial growth of crowdfunding and the liquidity shortage due to the financial crisis, led to a change in US legislation (Stemler 2013) and in 2011, a legislative proposal was developed to increase the access to capital for new and small ventures that came into force on April 5, 2012. The primary objective of this "Jumpstart our Business Startups Act" (JOBS Act) was to help new and small firms to raise equity capital more comfortably with a reduction in interest cost. The liberalization of the Securities Act of 1933 is heavily discussed in the legal literature of crowdfunding (e.g., Bradford 2012; Cohn 2012; Cumming and Johan 2013; Griffin 2012; Hazen 2012; Heminway and Hoffman 2011). However, legal provisions of crowdfunding are country-specific and very heterogeneous. In most countries, among others in the EU, the issuance of shares through equity crowdfunding is either prohibited or costly due to stringent legal requirements.

(ii) *Motivations of companies for crowdfunding*

Crowdfunding appeared as a blessing for the new ventures (Hemer et al. 2011) as it aids the promoters to reduce the funding gap in the early stage of their businesses when their own funds and love money (capital given by friends and relatives) are insufficient. So far, empirical works have identified several motives for choosing crowdfunding by startups and the young firms as well. For example, Belleflamme et al. (2013) identified three main reasons for companies that adopted crowdfunding. They are the collection of funds, the attainment of public attention, and receiving feedback for their products or services. Gerber et al. (2012) conducted semi-structured interviews with market participants and identified five categories of motivation such as financing, networking, self-affirmation, replication of success stories, and increased awareness of the product. Crowdfunding also motivates entrepreneurs to obtain funding in the early stages of a company's life cycle (Hemer et al. 2011).

Other incentives of crowdfunding include the speed and flexibility of the funding, little formal obligations, testing the product in the market, positive multiplier effects, positive signalling effects, and the use of the "wisdom of the crowd" for performing various company tasks (Hemer et al. 2011; Hienerth and Riar 2013; Macht and Weatherston 2014). Crowdfunding also offers the opportunity to the consumers to be investors. Crowdfunding investors are those people who greatly believe in the success of the company and its products or services. Hence, the company gets legitimacy from the market (Martin 2012) whether crowdfunding is successful, and at the same time, building a customer base. Notably, crowdfunding is not only a financing tool for companies but also a communication tool to facilitate better access to customers, more extensive press coverage, and higher interest from potential employees and others.

(iii) *Factors contributing to the success of crowdfunding*

As regards to the factors contributing to the success of crowdfunding, the empirical literature shows that companies for social causes have a higher potential for success in raising fund through crowdfunding. For example, Belleflamme et al. (2013) argued that non-profit organizations have higher credibility in fulfilling the investors' expectation compared to the profit-oriented organizations. To this tune, Lehner (2014) suggested harmonizing the crowdfunding and social entrepreneurship. Mollick (2014) examined archival data from the platform Kickstarter and found that the probability of a successful crowdfunding transaction decreases with the increase in the funding amount asked for and with the duration of campaigns for soliciting crowdfunding.

In addition, the likelihood of the success of crowdfunding is found to be associated with several factors such as the size of the social network used by fund seekers, the presence of a product video, and geographical proximity to capital (Frydrych et al. 2014; Giudici et al. 2013; Hekman and Brussee 2013; Mollick 2014; Saxton and Wang 2013). The positive influence of geographic proximity on funding success was also found in P2P lending markets (Burtch et al. 2013b; Lin and Viswanathan 2013). Moreover, emotional (Lin and Viswanathan 2013) and cultural (Burtch et al. 2013b) factors such as strong preferences for local products and services tend to associated with the funding success. Also, Mollick and Kuppuswamy (2014) found that successful capital seekers are very active in social media like Facebook, Twitter, and so on.

4.2.2 Crowdfunding Literature on Fund Providers

From the perspective of fund providers, crowdfunding literature tends to focus on attributes of the fund providers, social media, and signals given for crowdfunding. Below is a summary of notable works in this respect.

(i) *Attributes of fund providers*

Investors are critically important for the success of crowdfunding. However, empirical works reveal that investors participated in crowdfunding transactions are heterogeneous and mostly centers on the respective crowdfunding model (Lin et al. 2014). For instance, Allison et al. (2015) and Lin et al. (2014) found that investors are motivated not only by the financial factors but also by the social contribution of the company. Several other studies claimed that fund providers tend to have some similar attributes such as they are innovation-oriented, interactive, like to identify themselves with the company or with the product, and mostly interested in the financial result (Gerber et al. 2012). In addition, Hemer et al. (2011) identified that factors such as interest in using the product or service, the attainment of self-affirmation, and having fun are important inducement for the capital providers in undertaking crowdfunding investment.

(ii) *Social media*

The active involvement of the investors in social media is another critical factor for the investors to participate in crowdfunding transactions. Several studies examined the effects of social networks on the investment decision in crowdfunding. Undoubtedly, social media help reduce information asymmetry and enhance funding possibility (Everett 2010; Freedman and Jin 2014; Lin et al. 2013; Liu et al. 2013; Zvilichovsky et al. 2013). However, social media may induce investors' to be free riders (Herzenstein et al. 2011; Lee and Lee 2012; Yum et al. 2012; Zhang and Liu 2012). However, Herzenstein et al. (2011) argued that the herding behavior in crowdfunding transactions is strategic and rational because it can reduce the default rates of loans. Kuppuswamy and Bayus (2013) noted that factors such as investments by family and firm's promotional activities have a positive influence on the funding process, particularly at the beginning and at the end of the funding. However, Lin et al. (2014) and Garton et al. (1997) identified different prototypes of investors that seem to react differently to social influences and signals of quality as well.

(iii) *Signals from peers in crowdfunding*

Signaling tends to be very common in crowdfunding transactions. Investors are likely to interact one another frequently, and they convey messages to subsequent capital providers (Burtch et al. 2013a; Koning and Model 2013; Smith et al. 2013; Wash 2013). Ward and Ramachandran (2010) identified a positive association of an investment decision with the results of similar, already-funded projects, the actions of other capital providers, popularity rankings, and blog posts. Qiu (2013) also found that blog posts (word-of-mouth effect measured by tweets), media coverage and platform features promote crowdfunding transactions. Kim and Viswanathan (2013) studied crowdfunding in the mobile application market and found that early investment by experts provides a positive signal to the crowd for subsequent financing. Furthermore, recommendations from friends and acquaintances also influence funding probability (Lin et al. 2013; Liu et al. 2013). However, Hildebrand et al. (2013)

documented that endorsements from peers are only understood as credible signals when the endorsements are linked with investments of the respective person.

4.2.3 Literature on Crowdfunding Platforms

Crowdfunding platform bridges the gap between the fund seekers and investors in crowdfunding transactions. Besides, it acts as information, communication and execution portal by ensuring a standardized process. It can lessen information gap and the risks for the participants (Haas et al. 2014). Platforms can also enable market makers to build trust (Burtch et al. 2013a; Greiner and Wang 2010). Wash and Solomon (2014) found that investors tend to contribute higher amounts when crowdfunding platforms tag a return rule for financing a project. However, Wash and Solomon (2014) recommended the return rule technique should be used only by platforms that offer high-risk projects to the crowd.

Maeschle (2012a) studied the first come, first served funding principle often used by the crowdfunding platforms. This model implies a hard end of the funding as soon as the funding limit is reached. However, unless there is a shortage of aggregate demands, this method does not lead to optimal resource allocation. This is because the quick and well-informed crowds can prevent spreading of company shares by investing large sums. They can also intentionally take the controlling stake of a company and replace the founders later. To reduce informational problem among capital providers, Maeschle (2012b) argued that platforms should publish fund seeking company's balance sheet, management quality (particularly team structure, education, and age), and business information such as firm size, legal form, ownership structure, industry, and location.

4.3 Avenues for Future Research

Crowdfunding is a disruptive innovation in entrepreneurial finance. The crowdfunding industry is still in an infant stage. Given the novelty of the concept, it demands more research from socio-economical, financial, behavioral, and regulatory perspectives. More studies also warranted from the standpoint of the investors, investee firms, and crowdfunding platforms. Here we outline some avenues for future research.

- Undoubtedly, crowdfunding reduces much of the screening problem associated with entrepreneurial finance as the crowdfunding platforms and a large pool of investors having diverse backgrounds do the screening of projects. However, it is not known how the moral hazard or enforcement problem would be addressed in crowdfunding technology. For instance, crowdfunding platforms may adapt conditional payment technique (funds will be realized step by steps) to reduce investors 'moral hazard. However, it does not reduce entrepreneurs' moral hazard and incentive problem. Thus, how to address the agency problem in crowdfunding transactions or for that matter assurance of the governance quality of the crowdfunding-backed firms could be a big issue for future research.

- The success of crowdfunding technology depends on the alignment of incentives among major parties involved in the financial transaction. A question thus arises how to align investors' incentives with fund seekers' (entrepreneurial firms) incentives? Can venture capitalists play an essential role in the alignment of incentives between interested groups? In addition, can the involvement of venture capitalist enhance the success of the crowdfund-backed firms by improving their quality of governance? Investigation of these issues would be an exciting contribution to the crowdfunding literature.
- It is observed that some funds are successful while many are not. This raises a question whether the success of funds is platform-specific, industry-specific or entrepreneur-specific. A platform-wise comparison of the success and failure of funds could be another interesting issue for future research. The above issue can also be investigated from cross-country perspectives. These would indeed assist policymaking institutions for the countries interested in crowdfunding.
- Crowdfunding is viewed as a compliment to venture capital finance. Thus, it demands identification of factors similar and dissimilar to venture finance. Legitimacy is an important issue in entrepreneurial finance. Thus, the issue is how do entrepreneurs institute and demonstrate legitimacy in this virtual, impersonal context?
- Crowdfunding is mostly an online phenomenon that is not free from cyber-attack and other fraudulent activities such as money laundering and terrorism financing. Therefore, the issue is how to design appropriate mechanisms to check such threats and dishonest practices?
- Crowdfunding could be a powerful tool to cater to the financing needs of the small firms in developing countries. However, developing countries tend to have a different set of cultural, economic, and institutional forces that suppress entrepreneurial activity and flow of funds. Opportunistic behavior is also prevalent in developing countries. So, how the developing countries can create a vibrant crowdfunding ecosystem in the midst of the opportunism? This could be another critical issue for the growth and sustainability of crowdfunding.

References

Akerlof GA (1970) The market for lemons: quality uncertainty and the market mechanism. Q J Econ 488–500

Allison TH, Davis BC, Short JC, Webb JW (2015) Crowdfunding in a prosocial microlending environment: examining the role of intrinsic versus extrinsic cues. Entrepreneurship Theory Pract 39(1):53–73

Belleflamme P, Lambert T, Schwienbacher A (2013) Individual crowdfunding practices. Venture Capital 15(4):313–333

Bradford C (2012) Crowdfunding and the federal securities laws. Columbia Business Law Rev 1:1–150
Burtch G, Ghose A, Wattal S (2013a) An empirical examination of the antecedents and consequences of contribution patterns in crowd-funded markets. Inf Syst Res 24(3):499–519
Burtch G, Ghose A, Wattal S (2013b) Cultural differences and geography as determinants of online pro-social lending. Retrieved August 2016, from https://papers.ssrn.com/abstract=2271298
Christensen CM (1997) The Innovators dilemma: when new technologies cause great firms to fail. Harvard University Press, USA
Cohn S (2012) The new crowdfunding registration exemption: good idea, bad execution. Retrieved 15 July 2016 from http://papers.ssrn.com/sol3/papers.cfm?abstract_id=2066016
Cumming D, Johan S (2013) Demand driven securities regulation: evidence from crowdfunding. Venture Capital 15(4):361–379
Everett C (2010) Group membership, relationship banking and loan default risk: the case of online social lending. Retrieved 10 Apr 2017, from http://papers.ssrn.com/sol3/papers.cfm?abstract_id=1114428
Freeman RE (1994) The politics of stakeholder theory: some future directions. Bus Ethics Q 4(4):409–421
Freeman L (2004) The development of social network analysis: a study in the sociology of science. Empirical Press
Freedman S, Jin G (2014) The signaling value of online social networks: lessons from peer-to-peer lending. NBER working Paper No. 19820. Retrieved 15 May 2014, from http://www.nber.org/papers/w19820
Frydrych D, Bock A, Kinder T, Koeck B (2014) Exploring entrepreneurial legitimacy in reward-based crowdfunding. Venture Capital 16(3):247–269
Garton L, Haythornthwaite C, Wellman B (1997) Studying online social networks. J Comput-Mediated Commun 3(1). https://doi.org/10.1111/j.1083-6101.1997.tb00062.x
Gerber E, Hui J, Kuo P (2012) Crowdfunding: why people are motivated to post and fund projects on crowdfunding platforms. Retrieved from http://www.juliehui.org/wp-content/uploads/2013/04/CSCW_Crowdfunding_Final.pdf
Giudici G, Guerini M, Rossi-Lamastra C (2013) Why crowdfunding projects can succeed: the role of proponents' individual and territorial social capital. SSRN working Paper No. 2255944. Retrieved 29 Apr 2017, from http://ssrn.com/abstract=2255944
Greiner ME, Wang H (2010) Building consumer-to-consumer trust in E-Finance marketplaces: an empirical analysis. International Journal of Electronic Commerce 15(2):105–136
Granovetter M (2005) The impact of social structure on economic outcomes. J Econ Perspect 19(1):33–50
Griffin ZJ (2012) Crowdfunding: fleecing the American Masses. Case Western Reserve Journal of Law, Technology & the Internet. Retrieved from http://papers.ssrn.com/sol3/papers.cfm?abstract_id=2030001
Haas P, Blohm I, Leimeister J (2014) An empirical taxonomy of crowdfunding intermediaries. Retrieved 20 July 2017, from http://www.crowdinvesting.jura.uni-muenchen.de/dokumente/crowdfundingintermediaries.pdf
Hazen T (2012) Crowdfunding or fraudfunding? Social networks and the securities laws—why the specially tailored exemption must be conditioned on meaningful disclosure. NCL Rev 90:1735–1769
Hekman E, Brussee R (2013) Crowdfunding and online social networks. Retrieved 15 May 2017, from http://www2.mmu.ac.uk/media/mmuacuk/content/documents/carpe/2013-conference/papers/entrepreneurship/Erik-Hekman,-Rogier Brussee.pdf
Hemer J, Schneider U, Dornbusch F, Frey S (2011) A snapshot on crowdfunding. Retrieved 5 Oct 2017, from http://www.legalefiscale.it/wp-content/uploads/2016/09/StudioCrowdfundig.pdf
Heminway J, Hoffman S (2011) Proceed at your peril: crowdfunding and the securities act of 1933. Tenn L Rev 78:879–972

Herzenstein M, Dholakia UM, Andrews RL (2011) Strategic herding behavior in peer-to-peer loan auctions. J Interact Mark 25(1):27–36

Hienerth C, Riar F (2013) The wisdom of the crowd vs. expert evaluation: a conceptualization of evaluation validity. Paper presented at 35th DRUID celebration conference, Barcelona, Spain, June 17–19. Retrieved from http://druid8.sit.aau.dk/acc_papers/im4odl75ix421p8l11ry1qg6gko8.pdf

Hildebrand T, Puri M, Rocholl J (2013) Adverse incentives in crowdfunding. SSRN working Paper No 1615483. Retrieved 10 May 2017, from http://papers.ssrn.com/sol3/papers.cfm?abstract_id=1615483

Jensen MC, Meckling WH (1976) Theory of the firm: managerial behavior, agency costs, and ownership structure. J Financ Econ 3(4):305–360

Kappel T (2009) Ex-ante crowdfunding and the recording industry: a model for the US. Loyola Los Angeles Entertainment Law Rev 29(3):375–385

Kim K, Viswanathan S (2013) The experts in the crowd: the role of reputable investors in a crowdfunding market. SSRN working Paper No. 2258243. Retrieved 15 July 2017, from http://ssrn.com/abstract=225824

Koning R, Model J (2013) Experimental study of crowdfunding cascades: when nothing is better than something. SSRN working Paper No. 2308161. Retrieved 30 Aug 2017, from http://papers.ssrn.com/sol3/papers.cfm?abstract_id=2308161

Kuppuswamy V, Bayus BL (2013) Crowdfunding creative ideas: the dynamics of project backers in Kickstarter. UNC Kenan-Flagler research Paper No. 2013–15. Retrieved 20 June 2017, from http://dx.doi.org/10.2139/ssrn.2234765

Lee E, Lee B (2012) Herding behavior in online P2P lending: an empirical investigation. Electron Commer Res Appl 11(5):495–503

Lehner O (2014) The Formation and interplay of social capital in crowdfunded social ventures. Entrepreneurship Reg Dev 26(5–6):478–499

Leland H, Pyle D (1977) Information asymmetries, financial structure, and financial intermediation. J Financ 32:371–387

Lin M, Viswanathan S (2013) Home bias in online investments: an empirical study of an online crowd funding market. SSRN Working Paper No. 2219546. Retrieved 10 Apr 2017, from http://papers.ssrn.com/sol3/Delivery.cfm?abstractid=2219546

Lin Y, Boh WF, Goh KH (2014) How different are crowdfunders? SRRN working Paper No. 2397571. Retrieved August 25, 2017, from http://papers.ssrn.com/sol3/Papers.cfm?abstract_id=2397571

Lin M, Prabhala NR, Viswanathan S (2013) Judging borrowers by the company they keep: friendship networks and information asymmetry in online peer-to-peer lending. Manage Sci 59(1):17–35

Liu D, Lu Y, Brass D (2013) Friendships in online peer-to-peer lending: pipes, prisms, and social herding. SSRN working Paper No. 2251155. Retrieved 30 July 2016, from http://papers.ssrn.com/sol3/papers.cfm?abstract_id=2251155

Macht S, Weatherston J (2014) The benefits of online crowdfunding for fund seeking business ventures. Strateg Change 23(1–2):1–14

Maeschle O (2012a) Rationing of excessive demand on crowdinvesting-platforms. Applied economic theory working Paper No. 126. Retrieved 10 Apr 2017, from http://www.econstor.eu/handle/10419/74657

Maeschle O (2012b) Which information should entrepreneurs on german crowdinvesting- platforms disclose? Applied economic theory working Paper No 127. Retrieved 10 Apr 2017, from http://www.econstor.eu/handle/10419/74650

Martin T (2012) The Jobs Act of 2012: balancing fundamental securities law principals with the demands of the crowd. SSRN working Paper No. 2040953. Retrieved 10 Apr 2017, from http://papers.ssrn.com/sol3/papers.cfm?abstract_id=2040953

Mollick E (2014) The dynamics of crowdfunding: an exploratory study. J Bus Ventur 29(1):1–16

Mollick E, Kuppuswamy V (2014) After the Campaign: outcomes of crowdfunding. UNC Kenan-Flagler research Paper No. 2376997. Retrieved 15 May 2016, from http://papers.ssrn.com/sol3/papers.cfm?abstract_id=2376997

North DC (1990) Institutions, institutional change, and economic performance. Cambridge University Press, London

Podolny JM, Baron JN (1997) Resources and relationships: social networks and mobility in the workplace. Am Sociol Rev 62(5):673–693

Qiu C (2013). Issues in crowdfunding: theoretical and empirical investigation on Kickstarter. SSRN working Paper No. 2345872. Retrieved 15 May 2015, from http://papers.ssrn.com/sol3/papers.cfm?abstract_id=2345872

Saxton GD, Wang L (2013) The social network effect: the determinants of giving through social media. Nonprofit Voluntary Sect Q 43(5):850–868

Valenzuela S, Park N, Kee KK (2009) Is there social capital in a social network site? Facebook use and college students' life satisfaction, trust, and participation. J Comput-Mediated Commun 14(4):875–901

Spence M (1973) Job market signaling. Q J Econ 87(3):355–374

Smith S, Windmeijer F, Wright E (2013) Peer effects in charitable giving: evidence from the (running) field. Econ J. https://doi.org/10.1111/ecoj.12114

Stemler AR (2013) The Jobs Act and crowdfunding: harnessing the power—and money—of the masses. Bus Horiz 56(3):271–275

Ward C, Ramachandran V (2010) Crowdfunding the next hit: microfunding online experience goods. In: Workshop on computational social science and the wisdom of crowds at NIPS2010. Retrieved from http://people.cs.umass.edu/~wallach/workshops/nips2010css/papers/ward.pdf

Waldfogel J, Chen L (2006) Does information undermine brand? Information intermediary use and preference for branded web retailers. J Ind Econ 54(4):425–449

Wash R (2013) The value of completing crowdfunding projects. In: International conference on weblogs and social media (ICWSM), AAAI Press

Wash R, Solomon J (2014) Coordinating Donors on Crowdfunding Websites. In *Proceedings of the 17th ACM conference on computer supported cooperative work & social computing* (pp 38–48). Retrieved from http://www.rickwash.com/papers/return-rule.pdf

Wasserman S, Faust K (1994) Social network analysis in the social and behavioral sciences. Cambridge University Press, Cambridge

Wei W, Joseph K, Liu H, Kathleen M (2016). Exploring characteristics of suspended users and network stability on Twitter. Soc Netw Anal Min 6(51). https://doi.org/10.1007/s13278-016-0358-5

Wellman B (1988) Structural analysis: from method and metaphor to theory and substance, pp 19–61. In: Wellman B, Berkowitz SD (eds) Social structures: a network approach. Berkowitz. Cambridge University Press, Cambridge

Yum H, Lee B, Chae M (2012) From the wisdom of crowds to my own judgment in microfinance through online peer-to-peer lending platforms. Electron Commer Res Appl 11(5):469–483

Zhang J, Liu P (2012) Rational herding in microloan markets. Manage Sci 58(5):892–912

Zvilichovsky D, Inbar Y, Barzilay O (2013) Playing both sides of the market: success and reciprocity on crowdfunding platforms. In: *International Conference on Information Systems, Milan 2013*. Retrieved from http://aisel.aisnet.org/cgi/viewcontent.cgi?article=1031&context=icis2013

Chapter 5
Crowdfunding in Japan

5.1 Crowdfunding Activities in Japan

5.1.1 Introduction

Japan has always been unique in the world due to several factors such as intrinsic trust in the society, tacit knowledge, technological progress, and relationship-based governance framework that contributed to the growing Japanese economy and helped its people to live peacefully with a financial comfort over a prolonged period. Even today, Japan is viewed as one of the safest countries in the world in terms of domestic violence and social peace. As a result, crowdfunding looks somewhat different in Japan that it does in the Western countries, having its own features.

Crowdfunding started out in Japan as primarily a way to raise money for charitable causes under the Silent Partnership Act (tokumei kumiai) that restricted equity crowdfunding and provided crowdfunding platforms a zero tax facility on their incomes (fees or profits). It recently has been able to disentangle itself from that image by allowing equity crowdfunding in 2015. Notably, since the 1990s, Japan had a large number of non-profit organizations (NPOs) that contributed funds to many social enterprises; however, the first crowdfunding activity for business took place in late 2007 when Music Securities, a crowdfunding platform, helped a sake (wine) brewery firm raising capital through crowdfunding. Afterward, the Great Earthquake in Japan, which occurred in 2011 and affected many industries triggered crowdfunding as a financial tool to fund social enterprises, creative entrepreneurs, and small enterprises.

However, crowdfunding gained momentum in Japan in 2015 when the government asked the Financial Services Agency (FSA) to take initiatives to promote crowdfunding, and simultaneously reformed the Financial Instruments and Exchange Act (FIEA) to allow equity crowdfunding and to provide protection to investors. Now,

B. K. Adhikary et al., *Crowdfunding*, SpringerBriefs in Economics,
https://doi.org/10.1007/978-981-13-1522-0_5

crowdfunding is growing rapidly in Japan as an increasing number of entrepreneurs are turning to the web-based finance to materialize their creative ideas and dreams. Presently, at least 50 crowdfunding platforms are operating in Japan of which Music Securities, Campfire, Maneo, Readyfor, CyberAgent, and Makuake are noteworthy (Japan Sustainable Investment Forum 2014). According to Yanoresearch.com (2017), the crowdfunding industry in Japan reached to ¥74.5 bn in 2016, grew by nearly 98% from the previous year (2015).

5.1.2 Crowdfunding Models in Japan

On the heels of the Western models of crowdfunding, Japan introduced both lending-based and donation-based crowdfunding models to provide funding support to entrepreneurs, but the models were redesigned considering its cultural setup. For instance, Japan categorizes crowdfunding under the five types such as donation, purchasing, social lending, investment, and stock investment. Besides, Japanese crowdfunding models provide emphasis on long-term relationship and follow the "stakeholder approach" to ensure trust and transparency between crowdfunding platforms, fund suppliers, and borrowers.

In Japan, the donation-type crowdfunding includes both conventional online donation sites and community foundations. It also includes non-profit financial institutions, popularly known as NPO banks. According to JSIF (2016), there are at least twenty-five (25) NPO banks providing funding supports for social enterprises in Japan. By contrast, purchase-type crowdfunding appeals investors to pre-purchase products that have much social attention such as filmmaking, craft making, animation, and sports. A famous crowdfunding platform in this respect is CyberAgent, Inc. that was established in August 2013 to provide funding support for journalism and filmmaking.

On the other hand, the social lending-type crowdfunding is similar to P2P lending as practiced in the Western countries. Prominent examples of P2P crowdfunding platforms in Japan are Campfire and Maneo. Stock investment-type crowdfunding is mainly equity crowdfunding wherein investors can invest and trade their funds with the help of crowdfunding platforms, whereas the investment-type crowdfunding is an association-based crowdfunding platform that campaigns funds for entrepreneurs for a fee. A great association-based crowdfunding platform is Music Securities.

Notably, unlike the Western models of crowdfunding which is basically "a one-shot approach for getting fees" from the investors and entrepreneurs, Japanese crowdfunding models focus on building a long-term interest among fundraisers, fund suppliers, and intermediaries (crowdfunding platforms). Hence, Japanese crowdfunding model is viewed as a "relationship-based crowdfunding model" that is oriented to generate benefits for the community or stakeholders (platforms, investors, and financial institutions) both in the short and long-term.

For instance, Music Securities incorporated local banks and government officials from City Office in its lending model to find attractive candidates and to receive funding supports as well, besides its registered common investors (Details of Music Securities are discussed in Sect. 5.2). Similarly, Campfire stresses on "democratization of funding" by creating "cryptocurrency" (a digital or virtual currency that uses cryptography for security) and "polka" (a digital P2P payment service) to offer various incentives to investors at a reduced cost. Likewise, Maneo platform links Japanese retail investors with small and medium-sized entrepreneurs both in Japan and abroad on online. It also offers a franchise scheme for anyone interested in crowdfunding to build and expand Maneo's family. Below is a diagram that shows Maneo's business model and flow of funds (Fig. 5.1).

There are several key features in Maneo's crowdfunding model. First, there is no need for the investors to be an accredited investor and they have no limitations on the amount of investment. Second, investors put equity into Maneo in the form of loans; hence, they do not become shareholders of Maneo. Third, if Maneo makes a profit on a venture, investors of that venture are entitled to receive a share of the profits (i.e., interest @ 5–8% per annum). However, when Maneo gets a loss on the investment (i.e., borrowers become bankrupt, and there is a loss of capital), investors need to bear the capital loss. Finally, Maneo's franchisees can use the funds outside of Japan; even the funds are raised in Japan.

5.1.3 Growth of Crowdfunding in Japan

The growth of crowdfunding in Japan has been a little bit slower compared to its counterpart the US, the UK, and China. Figure 5.2 portrays the growth of crowdfunding in Japan over the period 2013-2017. According to Fig. 5.2, the crowdfunding industry grew from ¥12478 million in 2013 to ¥74551 million in 2016. During this time, the industry grew by nearly 81% on an average while it achieved a 98% rate

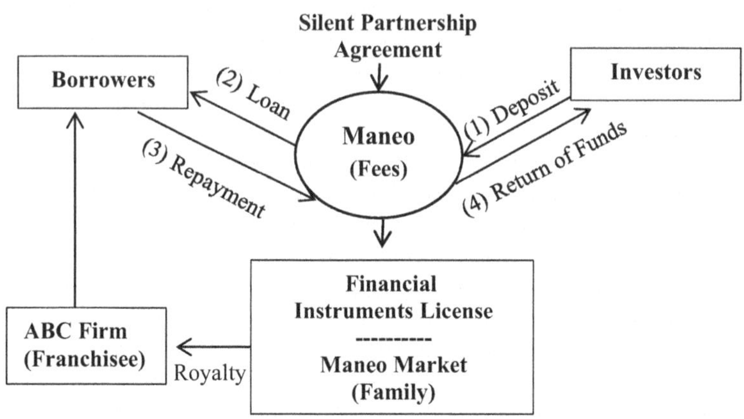

Fig. 5.1 Maneo's crowdfunding model *Source* Authors' construction from Maneo.jp

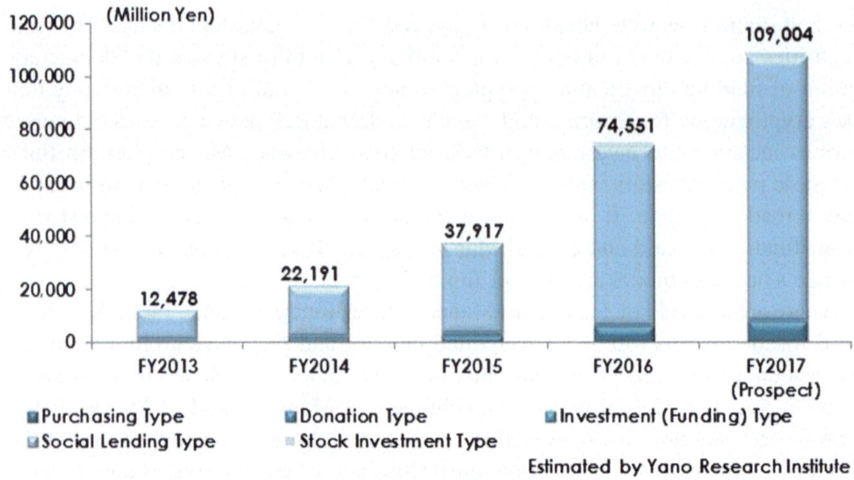

Fig. 5.2 Growth of crowdfunding in Japan (2013–2017) *Source* Adapted by authors from yanoresearch.com (2017)

of growth in 2016 against the previous year (2015). The industry expects to reach ¥109 bn in 2017 (yanoresearch.com 2017) According to statistia.com (2017), Japan's crowdfunding (transaction value) is expected to show an annual growth rate of 64.9% over the period 2017-2021, resulting in the total amount of ¥1515 bn in 2021.

As regards to the growth of crowdfunding by types, social lending-type crowdfunding tends to hold lion share of crowdfunding in Japan. In 2016, it holds 90.3% of total crowdfunding while the purchasing-type crowdfunding holds 8.4% at the same time. Other types of crowdfunding jointly capture 1.6% of the total crowdfunding wherein the stock investment-type crowdfunding bags merely 0.10% in 2016 (Fig. 5.3).

As regards to the growth of crowdfunding in Japan, it is worth to note that until 2011 Japanese people viewed crowdfunding platform as a charity site asking for funds for philanthropic activities. The 2011 Great Earthquake changed Japanese peoples' mindset for crowdfunding which triggered the social lending-type crowdfunding for many startups and small firms in Japan. As previously mentioned, the Silent Partnership Act allowed only donation-type crowdfunding in Japan. However, with the reform of FIEA in 2015, Japan introduced the concept of "small amount e-solicit business operator" and encouraged equity crowdfunding. In FIEA, e-soliciting has been defined as soliciting through websites and emails where an investor can invest yearly up to ¥0.50 million in a firm, and the investor's cumulative investment should be less than ¥100 million per year.

Importantly, in 2015, the Prime Minister, Shinzo Abe, assigned a project to the Financial Services Agency (FSA) to achieve economic growth in the startups by promoting equity crowdfunding. However, equity crowdfunding platforms required registration with the FSA besides the restrictions imposed by FIEA. As a result, equity

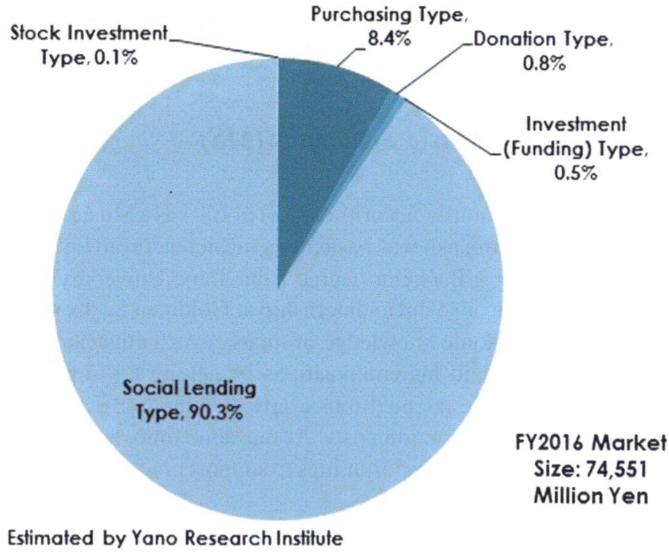

Fig. 5.3 Growth of crowdfunding by types (2016) *Source* Adapted by authors from yanoresearch.com (2017)

crowdfunding has not taken off to the extent desired by the ministers. By contrast, the P2P crowdfunding is rapidly increasing in Japan to cater to the financing needs of the creators.

Another important feature for crowdfunding in Japan is that Japanese entrepreneurs (creator) tend to have a huge responsibility for their products compared to the entrepreneurs in foreign countries. In Japan, the failure to do business or failure to produce expected results is viewed as entrepreneur's inefficiency in carrying out the business. Also, it becomes challenging for a failure entrepreneur to obtain funds next time for his projects. Thus, entrepreneurs who only have high commitments are likely to seek financial support from crowdfunding platforms. This, in fact, indicates why the early-stage company investments in Japan are small and conservative compared to other advanced countries (Morita 2016).

Simultaneously, the Japanese crowdfunding platforms tend to become very careful to check the idea of the creators in order to protect their trust and image with the registered investors and other stakeholders. This indicates that Japanese crowdfunding platforms implicitly assume the risk of business failures, besides the entrepreneurs. Therefore, they exercise "due diligence" approach to screening a proposal for crowdfunding. As a whole, due to the social culture, Japan's crowdfunding models exhibit somewhat a different style compared to the Western counterparts in intermediating finance to entrepreneurs.

5.2 Music Securities—A Case of Crowdfunding Platform in Japan

5.2.1 Background of Music Securities (MS)

Mr. Masami Komatsu set up music Securities (MS) in 2001 as a Music CD production and marketing company. Komatsu was basically a musician. From his childhood, he was fond of music. He got a Bachelor degree from Tama University and an MBA from Waseda University. He also did an internship at Goldman Sachs when he was a student. Therefore, he had some knowledge of finance. As a musician, he primarily wanted to keep a record of all his compositions by setting up a music company. Besides, his goal was to give talented music artists without a major label access to online funding to cover production costs. At the same time, he aimed to provide individual music fans investment opportunities to support pre-major debut musicians in their creative endeavors.

However, he did not have enough money to set up a company. Thus, he looked for external finance, especially from the banking system. Yet, the traditional banking system did not put a value on this idea because of higher uncertainties and competition in the music industries. Also, Mr. Komatsu did not have tangible assets to be placed in banks as security for granting loans. As a last option, he thought that he would ask his fans to contribute him some funds so that he can set up a music company. Assuming so, in the year 2001, he structured a fund "Bolero 1" and put up for sale compact discs as a music label. Fortunately, his fans contributed him some money as a donation, and with that, he established MS in Tokyo in 2001. Over time, he realized that many other businesses apart from music needed new financing sources for their creative activities or products. Therefore, he decided to expand funding to companies beyond music.

The company entered into the crowdfunding business in 2007 when the Development Bank of Japan (DBJ) introduced MS a sake (wine) brewery firm for giving possible financial help. Notably, sake production needs relatively a long time (in this case, it was two years) and DBJ found it difficult to lend money for such a long period. Mr. Komatsu accepted this sake brewery firm and used his social networks to raise money by launching a campaign in his own company's website. The scheme of fund contained (1) a token gift of sake bottle to all investors as soon as the fund reaches the target, and (2) extra bottles of sake if the number of investors becomes less than expected.

The scheme created an extra attraction especially for the sake lovers as they got opportunities for getting extra bottles, and the campaign became successful. Mr. Komatsu also invested a part of his music fund in this sake brewery firm. This was, in fact, the beginning of crowdfunding business in MS. The company has a branch in Osaka. It runs with a board of five members, all of them are graduated from reputed universities in Japan. Besides Mr. Komatsu, major shareholders of the company include Tokio Marine Capital (VC), Mitsubishi UFJ Capital (VC),

SMBC Venture Capital (VC), Dentsu Shizuoka Capital (VC), Hiroshima Capital (VC), Shigagin Lease Capital (VC), and Recruit Incubation Partners (VC).

In the year 2009, MS joined hands with the Japanese non-profit organization "Living in Peace" to launch LIP Microfinance Fund for Millennium Development Goals. With this, the company expanded beyond the national borders with "Cambodia ONE" that aimed at raising about $500,000 for Samic Microfinance, a Cambodian Microfinance organization that implements a rural credit programme known as Cambodian Health Committee Credit programme, which will fund an effort to reduce tuberculosis prevalence by reducing poverty. MS along with Living in Peace organizes investor study tours to investee MFIs and their clients so that the investors can know how their invested money has been used.

5.2.2 *Business Model*

MS follows a "relationship-based crowdfunding" approach with a long-term focus under the ambit of financial return-based crowdfunding framework. Under this model, a potential entrepreneur can directly apply for MS for crowdfunding and MS uses its own "due diligence" technique to reach a financial conclusion about the firm. Besides this direct application, MS uses two more techniques to get potential candidates for crowdfunding. First, it maintains a close relationship with the local banks. Local banks usually send those firms to MS that do not match with their lending strategies, because the firm has either insufficient capital/collateral or higher perceived risks associated with the firm, but have great potential to grow (Fig. 5.4). This implies that the first screening is done by local banks which saves entrepreneur's cost. Usually, local banks receive a fee for recommending firms to MS, but their objective is to extend a loan to this firm at a later stage when it grows and become bankable. Second, MS keeps a good relationship with the officials of City Office who also recommend good candidates for financing. Also, City Office provides some financial help to business proposals that fall under the regional growth strategies of the government (Note 1).

Once MS accepts a proposal, it posts the financial and non-financial information about the firms on its campaign page and asks its registered clients to supply funds. MS operates under the Silent Partnership Act in Japan. Thus, it acts just as an introducer of investors to funding firms, and the firms themselves manage the funds. MS, however, receives a fee (usually 5.7%) from the investors on their invested amount as a service charge. It also performs some public relations activities on behalf of the investee firm for a fee.

In this model, investors do not directly demand any guaranteed return on their investment but expect to get a good return in the long-term. However, key features of this model are that (i) MS initially performs the role of a quasi-monitor of the investee firm by injecting its own funds and simultaneously assuming the responsibility of its registered members that reduces moral hazards of the investor, (ii) local banks extends finance to firms backed by MS at a later stage, usually, a debt finance, and ensure

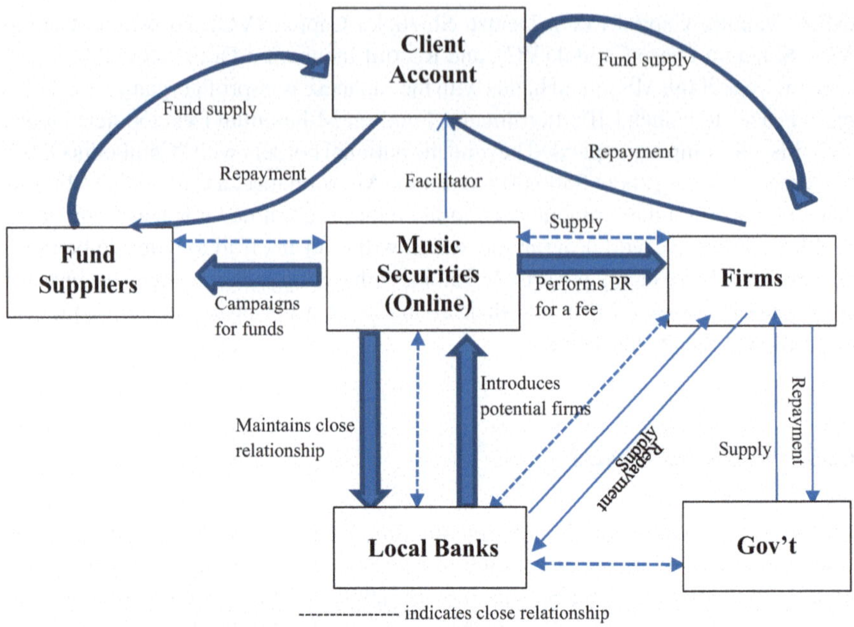

Fig. 5.4 Relationship-based crowdfunding model *Source* Authors' construction

the governance of the firm by becoming a quasi-monitor, and (iii) local government also provides finance to the MS-backed firm at a lower cost when it carries a national interest. As a whole, this model centers on the long-term relationship among different stakeholders to achieve a common goal, i.e., promotion of entrepreneurship and gaining profits in the long-term. We termed this model as a "relationship-based crowdfunding model" backed by "stakeholder theory." Figure 5.4 summarizes the MS's crowdfunding business model.

5.2.3 *Key Performance Statistics*

With the introduction of sake brewery firm in 2007, MS helped to raise 256 funds for 148 firms as of July 2014, of which 174 funds are in operation, and 82 funds are repaid to the investors with a success rate, 81% (Table 5.1). At present, MS is collaborating with 21 local banks to get potential firms for crowdfunding. Notably, MS has around 70,000 registered members who contribute to the firms campaigned for crowdfunding. The size of funds that MS raised for the firms varies mostly, ¥15.36 million on average with a minimum of ¥0.53 million, and a maximum of ¥200 million. Similarly, the subscription amount (in unit) varies by funds although the usual amount per unit is ¥10000.

Table 5.1 Descriptive statistics of firms backed by MS

As of July 4, 2014 (obtained from MS's Website)			
Number of investee firms	148	Number of collaborations with Chamber of Commerce	2
Number of funds	256	Number of funds given to music industry	>50%
Number of funds successfully repaid to investors	82	Average Size of Fund (¥ mil.)	15.36
Number of funds that produced fewer returns to investors than expectation	16	Funding period	3-10 years
Number of funds currently managed	174	Amount per unit (Depends on size of funds)	¥10000 (usually)
Number of collaborative local banks	21	Number of registered members (investors) (approx.)	70000

Source authors' construction from the website of MS, retrieved on July 4, 2014

With respect to the age of the suppliers of the fund, approximately 56% of the total fund suppliers belong to the age group of the 30 s and 40 s of which nearly 19% are women. By contrast, nearly 9% of the fund suppliers belong to the ages within the 20 s, whereas around 18% goes to the people over 60s (Table 5.2). Importantly, 50% of the fund suppliers are found to be company employees followed by self-employed persons, housewives, and students who collectively account for nearly 24% (Fig. 5.5). In addition, approximately 23% of the fund suppliers live in Tokyo followed by Kanagawa that accounts for almost 11%.

As regards to the return on funds, a definite conclusion cannot be made because many funds are yet to mature when we conducted this study. However, based on the reported data of 93 funds in the MS's website, it is found that approximately 58% of the total funds generated a positive return between 0 and 10% and nearly 8% of

Table 5.2 Fund suppliers' age

Age (years)	Sex		
	Male (%)	Female (%)	Total (%)
20<	0.17	0.06	0.23
20s	5.93	2.89	8.82
30s	19.51	9.37	28.88
40s	17.23	9.29	26.52
50s	11.77	6.19	17.96
60s or more	12.19	5.39	17.58
Total	66.80	33.19	99.99

Source authors' construction from the website of MS, retrieved on July 4, 2014

Fig. 5.5 Fund suppliers' by professions

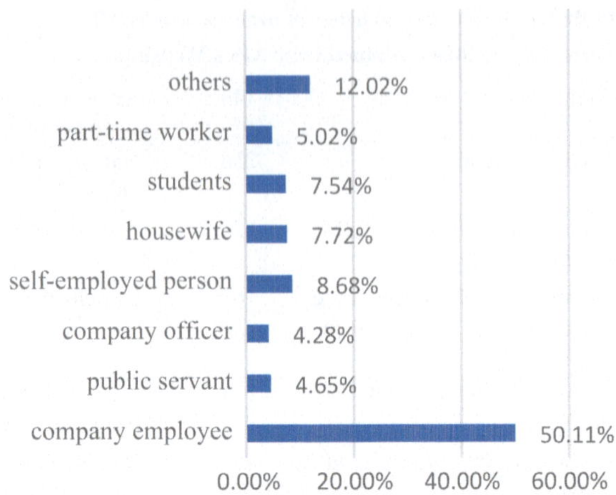

the funds have a yield above 10%. By contrast, nearly 13% of the funds demonstrate a negative return between 0 and 10%, and there are few outliers (Fig. 5.6). In this respect, it is worth to note that although the numerical returns of many funds are not seemingly attractive but their real rate of returns are very high if the number of jobs created by these funds are considered.

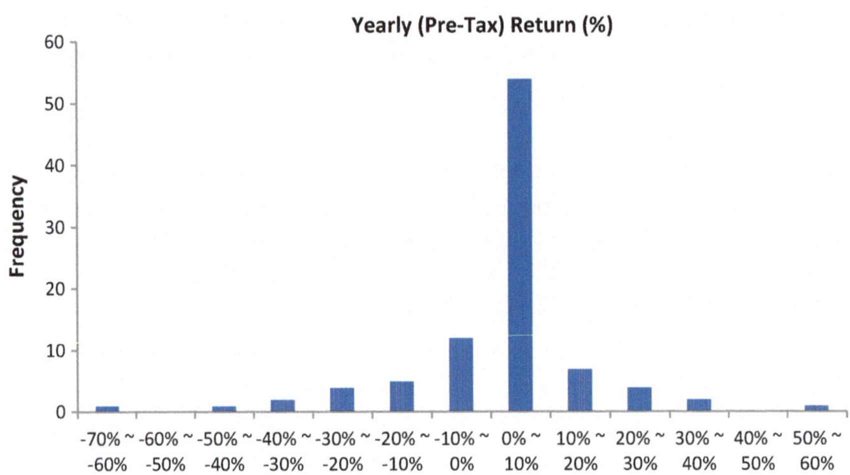

Fig. 5.6 Return on funds *Source* authors' construction from the website of MS, retrieved on July 4, 2014

5.2.4 Future Plans

MS is more than ready to face a new challenge. It plans to expand its operations in the Latin American and Caribbean region in industries like sake breweries, music, agri-businesses, and professional sports teams. It is also interested in e-book content, wineries, and investments in businesses related to tangible and intangible cultural heritage. MS is also planning to transfer Japanese business owner's skills and expertise to the Latin American and Caribbean region as it has established a comprehensive network of farmers and brewers through its fund businesses.

Also, since MS runs its own music label, it is interested in introducing Latin American and Caribbean musicians to the Japanese market. In Europe and USA, MS wants to explore the possibilities of funding from a growing number of savvy internet investors. The company believes that its model of business is viable even beyond the context of the Japanese market.

MS has also considered making equity investments in foreign microfinance institutions to participate in their corporate governance and introduce its micro-investment platform as their alternative funding source. Future funding for MS may come through possible capital increases through third-party allotments and possibly an IPO in Japan.

5.2.5 Lessons

The crowdfunding model used by the MS is relationship-based, forward-looking and long-term. It centers on stockholder theory. It heavily relies on the relationship of the local banks and officials of the local city office to solicit good firms, besides receiving a direct application from the entrepreneurs. Through this practice, MS substantially reduces transaction costs (time and labor) in screening the applicants, as the local banks already do the first screening. Then, MS applies its own due diligence and assesses the financial requirement of the firm. This double checking system, in fact, reduces investors' moral hazard problem and increases their incentives to become a long-term partner of the investee firm.

At the first stage, MS acts as a quasi-monitor of the firm, however, at a later stage, local banks also perform the role of a quasi-monitor when they extend loans to MS-backed firms. This joint monitoring system, although informal by type, reduces moral hazards of the investor further. Most importantly, local government also play a supportive role in providing finance to the firm at a lower cost, when it falls under the government policy of regional growth. This implies that local banks, MS (as an intermediary), entrepreneurial firms, general investors, and government officials co-operate each other in promoting finance to entrepreneurial firms and they become implied partner to get income in the long-term.

This system, in fact, reflects many characteristics of the previous "main bank system" of Japan that greatly contributed to the country's growth during its "Hey

Day" period. On the perspective of return on funds, it is very difficult to provide a particular comment right now as the industry is very new and many funds are yet to mature. However, the available data prove that firms that received funding supports through MS have a positive return in the maximum cases and the actual returns of the funds are much higher in a real term.

MS's success can be attributed to the fact that the company has stuck to its original business model despite having expanded to other industries and other countries. By specializing in online transactions through its platform, Securite, MS also achieves cost-effectiveness. Notably, this relationship based crowdfunding model draws particular attention to the policy-making institutions in developing countries as their main financial players face a systematic problem in intermediating finance to a large number of small firms and startups (discussed in Chap. 6). However, developing countries should not replicate this model naively, as trust in developing countries is seemingly fragile, indicating enough rooms for opportunisms and fraudulent behaviors.

In the final analysis, the difference between MS and other crowdfunding platforms is the relationship between investors and investees, which goes beyond financial returns. In a poll with 964 of its investors in sake brewers, MS found that 58% invested because they like sake and want to support it. In music, being financed by fans gives the partnering investees a definite feeling that it is different from other conventional financial institutions, Mr. Komatsu recalls.

5.3 SABAR Restaurant- a Case of Crowdfund-Backed Firm

Does the name Mr. Takanobu Migita ring a bell? Well, he is the owner of SABAR restaurant, which is in the business of trading of Saba (mackerel), the manufacturing and sale of products of Saba and the supervision and management of the SABAR restaurant. Mr. Migita obtained crowdfund from Music Securities in December 2013 as an alternative source of funding his business. The company raised three funds to open three SABAR restaurants in Fukushima, Tenma (Osaka) and Tokyo. Now, the company owns 12 SABAR restaurants in Japan with an overseas branch in Singapore. The company plans to conduct IPO in 2019. SABAR exemplifies a successful case of crowdfunding in Japan (Note 2).

What is SABAR?

The name "SABAR," takes on a special meaning. It is made up of a combination of two words, "*saba*" and "bar." The word "*saba*" means "mackerel" in English. Mackerels are surface-dwelling, migratory, blue fatty fish that are commercially important in Japan as a popular food fish in Japanese *washoku* and sushi.

SABA+BAR
= SABAR

The naming "SABAR" takes on a playful merge of the two words "*saba*" and "*bar*" to basically mean, a "mackerel bar." SABAR is a very popular restaurant based in Japan that serves a variety of mackerel-based dishes and menus. It is the only restaurant in Japan that centers one and only one particular fish, the *Saba*.

SABAR appeals to the health benefits of the mackerel, which contains DHA and EPA—important omega-3 fats that are good for health, skin, and beauty. Although SABAR started in Osaka, only top quality mackerel from the North Pacific Coast of Japan has a place on their *saba*-based dishes. SABAR uses only one special type of *Saba*, the *Toro-saba*. For a *Saba* to be called *Toro-saba*, the mackerel has to be: one, be fished from the North Pacific coast of Japan, two, contain over 21% fats, and three, weight over 550 g.

With such strict conditions on what *Saba* it uses, SABAR has grown very popular—growing and making branches across the country. Starting from Osaka, they have 12 branches in Japan including Tokyo, Osaka, Aichi, and Kobe. They have also branched overseas into making a restaurant in Singapore, which opened in 2016, July.

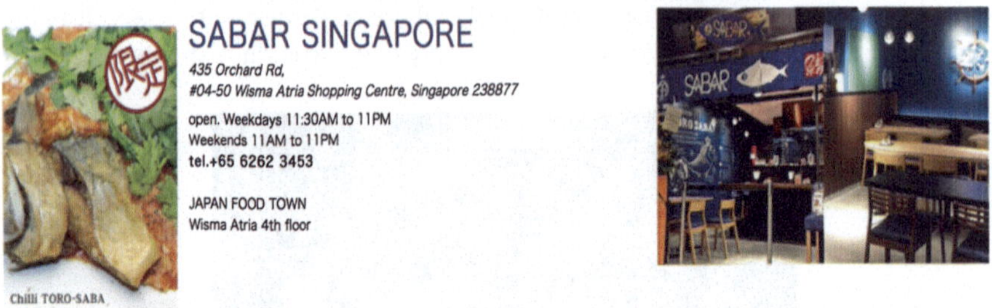

Introducing the Founder of SABAR: Takanobu Migita

The founder of SABAR, Takanobu Migita, was born in Osaka in 1974. After graduating high school at the age of 19, he started working at the fish section in super markets. Mr. Migita confesses that before working at the fish section, he disliked the taste of fish and never really ate it.

However, while working at the supermarkets, which included delivering fish to Japanese fish restaurants, he often got to taste fish for free. That was when he first felt that fish tasted delicious; so delicious that he realized he would never forget the taste.

At the age of 23, remembering his love for fish and thinking that he should experience new things, he moved to Australia to deepen his knowledge of fish. He started learning sushi and fish in a Japanese-owned sushi restaurant chain in Sydney after traveling to many places in Australia and brushing up on his English.

First starting as mere restaurant staff, his efforts led him into proceeding as factory chief, supervisor, onto area manager. He learned marketing and design through his experiences there. However, he soon realized that he aspired to work in Japan for Japan. At the age of 27, he quit his job in Sydney and went back to Japan in 2004.

The Birth of SABAR

At first, Mr. Migita felt sick of food-related jobs and did not feel like doing anything related to fish and food. After wandering about from job to job, at the age of 30, he decided to challenge himself by starting a small *izakaya*, or Japanese pub, in Osaka. To his surprise, out of the many menus that he served, the *saba* sushi that he served at the *izakaya* was the most popular hit. He realized that the *saba* sushi was the best meal he could make, and challenged himself further into starting a business based on selling just the *saba* sushi. He sent fax messages to many different companies writing: "if you buy one *saba* sushi, you will get another one for free." This was also a great hit, and Mr. Migita was soon very busy answering the orders on the crowded phone lines.

Soon after, in 2007, Mr. Migita established the "SABAYA COMPANY" and introduce mackerel sushi to supermarkets. He made efforts in branding by playing a theme song, "Sabababan," while selling the *Saba* fish. This resulted in many offers from department stores, and the SABAYA mackerel were sold at many different famous department stores.

At around the same time, Mr. Migita had heard that Hachinohe City in Aomori Prefecture was proceeding in branding their local "*Hachinohemae Oki* Mackerel."

Thinking that this was a great chance, Mr. Migita visited the site to present his ideas of selling mackerel in Kansai. This ultimately led him into being elected as the Ambassador of "*Hachinohemae Saba*". He soon was able to use these top- quality *saba* for his sushis.

While slowly moving towards success through SABAYA, one of Mr. Migita's friends, also an owner of a company suggested him start a mackerel-based restaurant because it was for sure to be popular and would generate lots of profits. Following his recommendation, Mr. Migita planned to open an exclusive Saba restaurant to manufacture a variety of high-quality Saba dishes such as Toro-Saba, which is a meaty kind of Saba and to become famous. However, he began to realize the limits of the possible expansion of such a business without sufficient funds that he lacked at that time. He spent four months for finding a reasonable way of raising funds to start a Saba restaurant.

Somewhere down the line, Mr. Migita came in contact with Mr. Yoshida, who was a member of the Chamber of Commerce and Industry of Toyonaka area in Osaka. He intimated Migita about the crowdfunding services provided by the firm Music Securities. Migita had watched a TV programme about Music Securities and was interested in obtaining funds for his restaurant through the means of crowdfunding.

Eventually, he obtained funds (¥17.88 million) through crowdfunding with the help of Music Securities and opened his first SABAR restaurant in Fukushima, Osaka at the beginning of 2014. The success of this restaurant led him to open the second restaurant in Tokyo. At this time, however, he planned to obtain half of the required money from crowdfunding and the remaining half from financial institutions. He got a success. The profits earned in this store led to the success in opening another store in Tenma, Osaka. Now, anyone can find SABAYA in department stores' underground food section, the *Depachika*, in the Hankyu department store, Takashimaya, Daimaru, etc. There is also an online store where anybody can buy *Toro-saba*, in which they can deliver it free.

The journey for Obtaining Crowdfunding

As previously mentioned, Mr. Migita's idea was to become famous by running a restaurant specializing in Saba that required lots of funds. Initially, he thought for applying for a bank loan, but soon he left that idea because he realized that the financial performance of his company at that time was not up to the mark and he felt that given the firm's financial situation it would be quite difficult for him to get a bank loan. Hence, following a recommendation from Mr. Yoshida, he thought of crowdfunding from Music Securities as an alternative source of funding his business.

However, as to the modus operandi of Music Securities, it did not provide any support to Mr. Migita in preparing its application for crowdfunds. Mr. Migita carefully prepared a business plan for SABAR and submitted the proposal to Music securities for consideration. When SABAR qualified for Music Securities crowdfunding, Music Securities provided a lot of support to Mr. Migita in raising funds. For instance, Music Securities provided Migita with opportunities to make his presentations many times, it requested reporters of Nikkei to visit the SABAR restaurants and introduced SABAR through its email magazine to 70,000 prospective customers. Besides, Music Securities organized parties with the fund suppliers of SABAR and then collected and analyzed questionnaires. Music Securities also prepared and uploaded web pages about the funds collected by SABAR through crowdfunding.

As to the structure of funds, one unit of investment was 30 thousand yen and the total required amount was 15 million yen excluding fees to Music Securities. The fund condition was that fund supplier would receive a return on profits for a subsequent five years. Also, the fund suppliers could get one set of Saba sushi per unit, when they invested. The campaign period was 16 weeks. Within 12 weeks, SABAR raised 17.88 million yen of which Music Securities received 2.88 million as a fee. The number of fund suppliers was close to 900 in total. Notably, Mr. Migita also obtained the second and third funds from Music Securities to expand his business, and at that time fees paid by investors and the fees paid by SABAR to Music, Securities were decreased a lot.

What is Attractive about SABAR?

As noted previously, Music securities did not provide any help to Mr. Migita in drafting his business proposal for crowdfunding. Mr. Migita carefully developed attractiveness of his proposed business. Some of the salient features of SABAR restaurant are as follows.

(a) Menu and Prices

As mentioned before, SABAR only serves meals centered on *Saba* and *Toro-saba*. Their customers come targeting the tasty high-brand *toro-saba* taken from Hachinohe, and Aomori, the "Hachinohe-shore *Saba*." It is hard to believe selling just one product can make a success. There are three main reasons why they are so popular. First, is the menu and prices.

The most eye-popping and popular dish on the menu is the "mega fatty *Saba* grill," which, considering that it measures larger than 30 cm, is quite inexpensive at the price of 1780 yen. The way it looks, is cooked, and feels, can be described to be something similar to the fatty tuna. This fatty *Saba* grill is big enough to satisfy more than two people, and most people order this first to share among themselves.

Aside from this striking menu, SABAR offers many different dishes of *Saba.* The dishes make up 38 menus in total. An attractive element of SABAR is how they cook *Saba* in forms of cuisines from many different countries. Although *Saba* is most well-known in Japan as sushi, Takanobu Migita creates a variety of *Saba* dishes by taking clues from the cuisines of many different countries. Mr. Migita wishes to take out the best from the S*aba* by challenging on new things. Here are a few of the most popular/most exciting menus from SABAR:

"*Negisa*" Saba skewer (250 yen)

Usually in Japan, skewers are made out of chicken, and it is called the "*negima*." SABAR uses that idea and turns it into "negiSA"—"sa" for "*Saba.*" They proudly serve it as one of their confident dishes.

"Bono! Siciliano! Sabano! Tomatoni-no!" (630 yen)

This cuisine, along with its playful name, is an Italian cuisine from the Sicilia Island. The oregano and tomato sauce matches well with the *Toro-saba* and black olives—a great meal to eat with wine and bread.

SABAR's Original "Fish'n Chips" (780 yen)

An all-time favorite loved by all customers who come to SABAR. What fish do people use for "fish and chips?" SABAR takes in the British menu and collaborate it with *Saba*.

"Toro-saba" Eskaveche (518 yen)

This is a creative dish taken from the cuisines from Peru. It is made up of frit-fried *Toro-saba* and marinated onions topped with spices.

Saba "Zukke" (680 yen) yen

The "*zukke*" is a popular Korean cuisine made of cold marinated vegetables and fish served in a mixed sauce. SABAR makes the *zukke* with avocado, yam, kimchi, and pickled *Saba.*

Restaurant Design and Themes

The second point of SABAR's success lies in each SABAR branch. As mentioned before, SABAR has 13 different branches across the world. Takanobu Migita was especially concerned about making each restaurant special. In such efforts, Mr. Migita made it so that each branch has a limited menu that can be ordered only at that restaurant. Some SABAR fans travel from far to taste all of the SABAR dishes available.

Another difference each restaurant has is apparent in the restaurant design itself. Each restaurant has a different concept and theme that makes people feels like they want to visit and see all of them. The restaurants are constructed according to their themes, and their designs take the customers into a different world. These efforts made hopes to, as Mr. Migita once mentioned, entertain the customers and give them a chance to enjoy *Saba* with their tongues, ears, and eyes.

The concept of the **Kyoto Karasuma SABAR** is the "*Saba Yashiki*." A y*ashiki* is described as an old, traditional Japanese-style mansion. Because Kyoto is a traditional city itself, the "*Saba Yashiki*" is designed to create a Kyoto- like environment where the unique culture can be felt. Their limited menu is the *"Toro-saba nabe,"* a Japanese hot pot with loads of *Toro-saba*.

The **Osaka Minamimorimachi SABAR** is designed to look like a "*Saba* aquarium." If you step into the restaurant, you feel like you yourself is a *Saba* or fish, swimming freely in the ocean. The wallpapers are colorfully painted in ocean colors and designs of fish swimming around. Their limited menu is the "*Saba*-1 Grand Prize," a *Toro-saba kushikatsu*. The *kushikatsu* is a deep- fried dish originated in Osaka. The Osaka Minamimorimachi branch also serves many different kinds of traditional foods from Hokkaido and Kyushu collaborated with the *Saba*.

The **Tokyo GEMS Omon** branch of SABAR is themed as the "*Ryugujyo*," or the "Undersea Palace." The *Ryugujo* is a famous fantasy place that takes an appearance in the well-known Japanese folk-tale, Urashimataro. The restaurant is designed to take you into that fantasy world as you pass through a red gate. People sometimes go to the restaurant cosplayed as Urashimataro or Otohime, the main characters of the Urashimataro folktale.

Following these special themes and designs, their limited menu is the "*Saba* Treasure Box," a plate filled with colorful sashimi, zuke, smoked, and marinated *Toro-saba*. They also have the *Toro-saba* soup.

(b) **Business Strategies**

According to Takanobu Migita's life story, Migita's opening of SABAR happened fast and a little bit unplanned. It was not like he spent years raising money, planning step-by-step for his new business. Starting from his small *izakaya*, his popular *Saba* sushi just progressed him into ultimately opening SABAR. When his friend suggested, he planned opening SABAR although he did not have enough money to start it. To obtain crowdfunding support from Music Securities, Mr. Migita simply narrated his past stories in the business plan and said that he does not have enough money to materialize his dream to become a famous businessman. Simultaneously, he explained how this

SABAR restaurant would bring unique and healthy dishes for Japanese people who are fond of eating fresh fish. He did not regard SABAR as a restaurant. Instead, he claimed that he is a maker of high-quality Saba. He primarily targeted business officials within 40–50 ages.

Mr. Migita, as playful he is with his love of fish, named his challenge on crowdfunding, the "Crowdfishing." The goal of "crowd fishing" was to take the mackerel, raise the mackerel, buy the mackerel, and eat the mackerel—basically doing everything needed for the *Saba* until it takes its place on the SABAR dishes. Since most of the *Saba* that is caught near the Japanese ocean is larval fish, Mr. Migita needs to raise them until they grow to be at least 550 g. When they are big enough to be sold, they are sold to EC site or store. "Crowdfishing" was needed to support the selling of good quality fish at a low price. Such naming and ideas of "Crowdfishing" attracted many supporters, and he had raised over 17 million yen within four months.

SABAR—A Place of Fun

The SABAYA Company was first taken up on media when Mr. Migita was delivering his sushi on his special *saba* motorcycle that wrote "*Sabike*." This playful mixture of words, "*saba*" + "bike" (motorcycles in Japan are often referred to as a bike) was what caught the attention of the media.

There are many places in SABAR's design that take on such fun ideas and elements, and are no doubt an important factor that contributed to SABAR's success. Following on with his "*Sabike*," he named his car "*Sabus*" (*saba* + bus,) and rides it around Japan introducing the benefits of mackerel. He also made many original characters, including the "*Saba Family,*" and the "*Saba* expert" who Migita modeled after himself, the "*Saba Hakase*."

Mr. Migita confessed that most of these unique ideas came from his wife who always says, “To have fun.” He said that when his work does not go well, his wife supports him with a bright, warm smile. His wife believes that work is determined by how fun it is. Whenever Mr. Migita seems troubled, she asks him, “are you enjoying your job right now?” She encourages Migita by telling him to have fun.

Some elements are also hidden in SABAR’s web address: www.sabar38.com. Why 38? Migita uses numbers playfully, in a unique way Japanese people “read” numbers to form words. 3 and 8 are read “*san*” and “*hachi*” in Japanese. In short, “*sa*,” and “*ha*,” when read, sounds like “*saba*.” SABAR starts lunch at 11:38, which, when reading carefully, reads “*ii saba*,” (1 is read “*i*” for “*ichi*,” so 11 reads “*ii*”) or “good mackerel.” The number 38 is all over Migita’s works, and he uses it as a fun entertainment of *Saba*.

Takanobu Migita also works in promoting the *Saba* itself. As mentioned before, he is the Ambassador of “Hachinohe-Okimae *Saba*.” The ambassador was created through a special movement to get people to know more about the Hachinohe S*aba*.

Mr. Migita focuses on sharing how tasty the *Saba* is by putting efforts in dietary education. He thinks that there are many people, especially children, who do not eat as much fish as Japanese people once did. Takanobu opened a “*Saba* sushi cooking class” for children to share how delicious *Saba* and fish can be. He also created a cooking class for women, cooking class for elders, and a special restaurant for children only. At the children's restaurant, "SABABIAN," children are able to learn how to serve and cook, as well as to train as a sushi chef.

Future Goals

Mr. Migita has many different plans to further promote *Saba*. He is now designing a new restaurant, "*Torosaba* Kitchen." The "Princess *Saba*" collaboration with JR West is actually another promotion of the "Princess *Saba*," which can be eaten raw safely because of its distinctive way of cultivation. They are cultivated so that the parasite anasakis are prevented.

However, Mr. Migita feels that the story of SABAR and the training of employees can be entry barriers to the expansion of his business. According to him, the existence of SABAR will be threatened if a big restaurant chain starts a similar business with low prices. Other restaurants can offer good Saba if they try. Therefore, cultivation of Saba can be a strong entry barrier. That is one of the reasons why SABAR is keen on the cultivation business. But, Mr. Migita does not plan to use investment type crowdfunding anymore. He stresses the fact that he has "graduated" from investment type crowdfunding to purchase type crowdfunding and he plans to make use of purchase type crowdfunding to cultivate Princes Saba.

Riding on the popular wave of "Cool Japan," Migita wishes to start many new SABAR branches overseas. Starting his human resources development plan called "*Saba* Academy," he wishes to teach people about the *Saba* so they can follow the "*Saba* Way." He wishes more people make "*Saba*" a source of their job, and that more "*Sabaryman*"s appear (Saba version of "salaryman."). He is designing many business models, aspiring for a "*Saba* Kingdom." He aims to chase his dreams with Mackerel in the future, making it a holding company, and listing shares. By 2019, Mr. Migita plans to conduct IPO, and by 2022, he dreams of opening 38 stores in total all over the world. In the end, his ultimate goal is 138 stores all over the world. "138" again, with its number play of "*iisaba*," describes exactly what Migita aims for—good mackerel known around the world.

Mr. Migita's View on Crowdfunding

Migita holds a very positive opinion towards crowdfunding, and, according to one of his interviews made in July 2015, he believes that there are six critical merits of crowdfunding:

(i) Crowdfunding allows you to create connections with your fans, with the people who agree with you, and with the people who support you. Not only is it helpful in raising the money, but crowdfunding allows you to open up your community and share with the people who wish your best.

(ii) Crowdfunding helps you understand your needs before you start doing your business. At first, Migita was unsure if SABAR would be a success. The crowdfunding method and its success helped him understand that people were indeed interested. Many things that are hidden shine light as possibilities through crowdfunding.

(iii) The method of crowdfunding itself assisted in the promotion of SABAR. Not many people at that time used this method when setting up a restaurant. Migita's unique idea caught the attention of the media, and many people came to interview him. This was a positive out turn for SABAR, and it had also helped SABAR to get known more by many people.

(iv) Crowdfunding allows business starters to raise a foundation of money without the need of returning it. This makes it easier for new companies to try many things. Migita says that this was why he was able to open three restaurants in such a short span of time.

(v) Even if one does not have much experience in business, they have a chance of attracting followers through an appeal to passion. Crowdfunding gives everyone an opportunity to be heard. For those who are inexperienced and are unsure and unconfident as to how they could start a business, crowdfunding provides light to a possible start.

(vi) Many new opportunities and jobs are introduced through the expanding of the community. Sometimes, this connects to new jobs that seem unrelated to the primary category. For example, Mr. Migita is now working on a collaboration with JR West through a new campaign, "*Princess Saba*." Although his business on SABAR is unrelated to the JR train company, crowdfunding had made it possible.

Notes

1. Information on Music Securities was obtained from an interview with officials of Music securities of its Osaka office in June 2014.
2. We visited Sabar Osaka restaurant in May 2015, interviewed Mr. Migita, and other staffs. Information presented in this report was obtained through interview and access to Sabar website.

References

Japan Sustainable Investment Forum (JSIF) (2014) 2013 review of socially responsible investment in Japan. http://japansif.com/2013review.pdf

Music Securities (2014). http://www.musicsecurities.com/

Maneo.jp (2017). https://www.maneo.jp/apl/contents/crowdfunding/eng

Morita H (2016) Crowdfunding in Japan: current regulation and the future of business. Available at SSRN: https://ssrn.com/abstract=2752312

Wisma A (2017) Rubbish eat rubbish grow: holy saba sets the bar sky high. https://www.rubbisheatrubbishgrow.com/2017/02/01/sabar-singapore

Sabar (2017). http://www.japanfoodtown.sg/stores/sabar/, http://sabar38.com/. Accessed July 2017

Yanoresearch.com (2017) Crowdfunding market in Japan: Key research findings, 2017. https://www.yanoresearch.com/press/press.php/001730

Yebisu M (2017) "Sabar—mackerel speciality restaurant." Yebistic! Japan (16 Feb 2017). https://yebisublog.wordpress.com/2016/01/13/sabar-mackerel-speciality-restaurant/

Chapter 6
Crowdfunding Potential in Developing Countries—A Case of Bangladesh

6.1 Introduction

Bangladesh mainly relies on the three distinct sets of financial intermediaries to cater to the financing needs of the entrepreneurs. These are the commercial banks, which broadly include state-owned, private, foreign, and development financial institutions that work under the direct control and supervision of the Bangladesh Bank (the central bank of Bangladesh), stock markets, and a number of NGOs those mainly operate in the rural financial market. A close review of the performance of these financial players explains why startups and small firms[1] in Bangladesh are systematically omitted from their attention.

6.2 Unleashing Problems of Traditional Finance

(i) ***The Banking System***

The banking system of Bangladesh comprises of fifty six (56) commercial banks including five (5) state-owned commercial banks (SCBs), thirty nine (39) private commercial banks (PCBs), nine (9) foreign commercial banks (FCBs), and three (3) development financial institutions (DFIs) (Bangladesh Bank 2016, Annual Report 2015–2016). These financial institutions follow Basel III guidelines for extending credits and determining the capital adequacy ratio (CAR) as well as the risk of the banks. They also follow the Bangladesh Bank's risk assessment guidelines which

[1] The definition of small firms varies across countries. In Bangladesh, small firm in the manufacturing sector is defined as an industrial undertaking with real assets of Tk. 5 to 100 million (excluding land and factory building) or having employees between 25 and 99. For other sectors, small firms are those that have real assets of Tk. 0.5 million to 10 million or employees between 5 and 25 (Ministry of Finance 2010).

B. K. Adhikary et al., *Crowdfunding*, SpringerBriefs in Economics,
https://doi.org/10.1007/978-981-13-1522-0_6

require the maintenance of higher cash flows, quality collateral, and sufficient capital, *inter alia*, for providing credits. Furthermore, all commercial banks require maintaining a certain percentage of their demand and time liabilities in the form of statutory liquidity reserve (SLR)[2] and cash reserve (CR) with the Bangladesh Bank to give protection to the depositors.

Apparently, this strong regulatory framework tends to increase the loan rationing behavior of the banking system and make them be "boundedly rational." Credits are also to be intrinsically rationed in developing countries such as Bangladesh due to the problem of information asymmetry and moral hazard (Stiglitz and Weiss 1981). In addition, the excessive reliance on the codified system of assessing risks prescribed by Basel principles expects to generate a "credit crunch" situation, especially for the small firms and startups. This becomes clear when the percentage of total loans given to the small firms in Bangladesh is analyzed. For instance, small firms received not even one percent of the total loans disbursed by the banking system over the last ten years, except for the case of the term loan given to them in the year 2004 (Fig. 6.1). Surprisingly, both the term loan and the working capital loan reduced to the lowest level in the year 2010, 0.04% and 0.05%, respectively, indicating a severe form of credit rationing. This also implies that either the banking system of Bangladesh lacks skilled officers who are able to assess credit risk for various entrepreneurial firms under uncertainties or it needs to follow the stringent regulatory framework that impedes to provide loans to small firms.

Another reason for not extending credits to the small firms could be grounded on the low return on assets (ROA) and high non-performing loans (NPLs) of the banking system, especially for the SCBs and DFIs that together hold 30.30% of the total industry assets and 33.30% of the total industry deposits (Bangladesh Bank 2016, Annual Report 2015–2016). This becomes clear from the analysis of ROA and

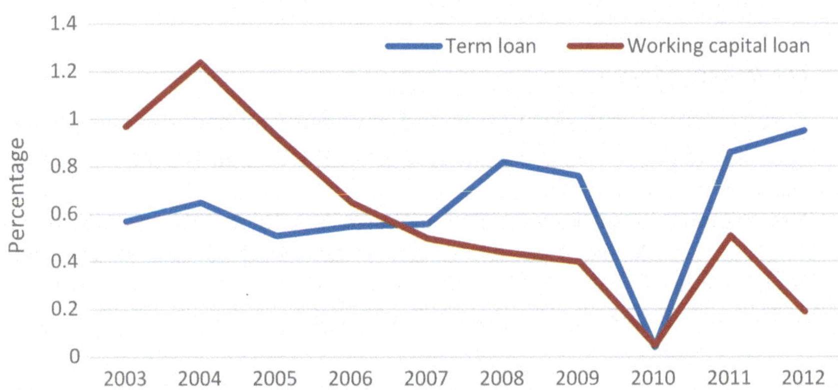

Fig. 6.1 Disbursement of loans to small firms *Source* Authors' construction from data given in scheduled banks statistics, various issues, Bangladesh bank

[2]At present SLR is 14% and CR ratio is 4%.

Table 6.1 NPLs and ROA by categories of banks

Year	NPL (% of total loans)					ROA (%)				
	SCB	PCB	FCB	DFI	All	SCB	PCB	FCB	DFI	All
2003	29	12.4	2.7	47.4	22.1	0.1	1.1	2.8	0.7	0.7
2004	25.3	8.5	1.3	42.8	17.6	−0.1	0.8	2.4	0.3	0.5
2005	21.3	5.6	1.2	34.8	13.5	−0.1	0.7	2.6	0	0.5
2006	22.9	5.4	0.8	33.6	13.1	0	1.2	3.2	−0.2	0.7
2007	29.8	5.0	1.4	28.5	13.2	0	1.1	3.1	−0.1	0.6
2008	25.4	4.4	1.9	25.5	10.8	0.7	1.1	2.2	−0.2	0.8
2009	21.4	3.9	2.3	25.9	9.2	1	1.3	3.1	−0.3	0.9
2010	15.7	3.2	3	24.2	7.3	1.1	1.4	2.9	−0.6	1.2
2011	11.3	2.9	3	24.6	6.1	1.3	1.6	3.2	0.4	1.4
2012	23.9	4.6	3.5	26.8	10	−0.6	2.1	2.9	0.2	1.8
2013	19.8	4.5	5.5	26.8	8.9	0.6	1.0	3.0	−0.4	0.9
2014	22.2	5.0	7.3	32.8	9.7	−0.6	1.0	3.4	−0.7	0.6
2015	21.5	4.9	7.8	23.2	8.8	0.8	1.0	2.9	−1.2	0.8

Source adapted by authors' from different Annual Reports, Bangladesh Bank

NPL data of the banking system of Bangladesh over the last 13 years (2003–2015) (Table 6.1).

According to Table 6.1, the banking system presently holds 8.8% NPLs (the year 2015) though it reached to 6.1% in the year 2011 (Bangladesh Bank 2016, Annual Report 2015–2016). Similarly, the ROA of the banking system reduced to 0.8% in 2015 although it had 1.2% in 2012, indicating apparently the decrease of banks' efficiency. Among the categories of banks, the SCBs and DFIs tend to perform poorly over the years by holding an alarming amount of NPLs (21.5 and 23.2% respectively, in 2015) with a poor and negative records of ROA (0.8 and −1.2% respectively, in 2015).

This indicates that NCBs and DFIs both either do not have sufficient skills to screen the borrowers properly and actively monitor their loan portfolios or they are directed by the government to disburse credits, the state-owned enterprises, in particular, without assessing risks. Notably, SCBs and DFIs together account for almost one-third of the total banking assets and deposits, and logically, they cannot take additional risks involved in financing the small firms because such an initiative would fuel their NPLs further and may bring financial mishaps in the country.

On the other hand, the PCBs and FCBs, which are relatively found in a better position in terms of curving NPLs and increase of ROA, they usually follow "branch banking"[3] and "selective credit policy" that discourage them to open branches in rural areas and disburse credits to the small firms exposed to business risks with a shortage of collateral. Obviously, under a free and a fair policy framework, the

[3]Under the branch banking, new branches are opened only in profitable areas..

Table 6.2 Stock markets performance in Bangladesh

Year	Dhaka stock exchange (DSE)				Chittagong stock exchange (CSE)			
	NLC	GSPI (%)	TV (%)	MC/GDP (%)	NLC	GSPI (%)	TV(%)	MC/GDP (%)
2005	−8	30	17	4	12	−6	7	65
2006	16	−22	35	6	1	10	6	59
2007	4	60	22	5	14	106	6	65
2008	13	40	40	9	11	14	9	130
2009	14	0	27	14	−21	52	12	148
2010	−29	104	89	16	8	78	11	239
2011	−1	−1	119	33	16	−37	11	430
2012	12	−25	141	29	14	−14	9	248
2013	14	−4	61	21	14	3	7	195

Source Authors' calculations based on data from Bangladesh Bank Quarterly (various issues), and Portfolios of CSE (various issues)

Notes

(a) *NLC* newly listed company, *GSPI* growth in general share price index, *TV* turnover velocity measured as annual stock turnover over GDP, *MC* Market Capitalization

(b) In 2004, the number of listed companies in DSE and CSE was 267 and 198, respectively

government cannot compel the PCBs and FCBs to provide credits to the small firms and startups.

The entire situations indicate that the banking system faces a systematic problem in providing finance to the small firms. Moreover, the main players in the system seem to be less resilient, highly distorted, fragmented and less competitive when their levels of NPLs and ROAs are considered.

(ii) ***The Stock Markets***

Bangladesh has two stock markets, the Dhaka Stock Exchange (DSE) and the Chittagong Stock Exchange (CSE), to channel funds to the entrepreneurs at all levels. When studying, these two stock markets reveal that the number of companies that sought capital via these markets during the last ten years is insufficient, and many enterprises delisted their status in some years (Table 6.2).

The principal market, DSE, demonstrates a rate of negative growth over the last couple of years when the growth in general share price index (GSPI) is taken into account. CSE also exhibits a similar trend, except for the year 2013. Furthermore, these two stock markets exhibit poor efficiency in allocating capital to the productive sectors when the stock turnover velocity (TV) and the number of newly listed companies are considered. However, the financial depth (measured as market capitalization over GDP) is found to be improved in the last couple of years.

As a whole, stock market exhibits dismal performance. Several reasons can be outlined in this regard. Firstly, Bangladeshis are usually risk-averse, as the bank deposits and investment in savings certificates issued by the government are found to account for almost 90% of the total finance in 2015 (authors' calculation from the data on Bangladesh Bank's Annual Report 2015 and Ministry of Finance). Secondly, people, in general, have ample doubts about the credibility of the stock markets due to the debacle occurred in the stock markets in 1997 and 2010 followed by the government's failures in arresting the perpetrators. Third, the country has only two rating companies and few security houses and investment banks that are yet to earn credibility and trust of the common investors. Fourth, the two stock exchanges require sufficient tangible assets and tracks of profits for the firms seeking capital. As a result, entrepreneurial firms or relatively younger firms seldom get opportunities to obtain funds from these two markets. Finally, Bangladesh does not have any separate markets for the startups or innovative firms that can provide opportunities to raise capital with minimum listing standards as is seen in the case of "Mothers" in Japan, "ChiNext" in China and "Kosdaq" in Korea.

(iii) ***Non-government Organizations (NGOs)***

Bangladesh has a number of NGOs that operate in the rural financial market to provide credits to the poor people. Grameen Bank is one of them that earned widespread recognition and subsequently received Nobel Prize in Peace in 2006. Notably, Grameen Bank targets socially and economically marginalized women to give them credits under a framework called "solidarity group lending".

According to Hoff and Stiglitz (1990), the group lending model creates sufficient moral pressure on the members of the group in screening the loan applicants and paying the installments spontaneously because the group is jointly held responsible for any lapses in the repayment of credit. As a result, it successfully mitigates the screening, incentives and enforcement problems associated with the rural finance.

Furthermore, it reduces transaction cost, risk premium and moral hazards in financial intermediations, which ultimately help increase profits of the loan giving institutions. This becomes clear from the analysis of the "cost of funds" and "return on investment" data of the Grameen Bank (Table 6.3).

As is observed from Table 6.3, the average cost of funds and return on loans for Grameen Bank are 7.54 and 17.49% respectively, showing an effective spread (return on loan—the cost of the fund) around a 9.93% on an average during the period 2003–2012. Indeed, this shows an impressive performance record for the Grameen Bank. However, the increasing trend of the cost of funds, which reached to 9.04% in 2012 from a 5.8% in 2003, and investment in fixed deposits in other financial institutions create doubt about the Grameen Bank's true profitability.

Importantly, Grameen Banks' fixed deposits that are put in other financial institutions provide a 10.29% risk-free rate of return on an average. Arguably, such fixed deposits may be considered as a cushion for the bank's operation, but this does not match with the working philosophy of NGOs. By regulation, Grameen Bank is also exempted from keeping statutory reserve requirements on its deposits and paying taxes on profits.

Nevertheless, a question arises—can Grameen Bank, or for that matter, other large NGOs take the responsibility of financing the small firms, especially when they are so successful in providing microcredits. We argue that at the present setting,

Grameen Bank and other NGOs cannot provide credits to the small firms because of the following reasons.

Firstly, Grameen Bank provides microcredit to the rural women mainly for income-generating activities that usually falls between $100 and $3500. However, entrepreneurial firms and startups require a relatively larger amount of funds for a longer time to advance their growth, which does not fall under the definition and range of microcredits.

Secondly, Grameen Bank uses a solidarity group lending model with a joint liability system where group members are usually known to each other, and some of them may be kin. Thus, even though there is no legal contract between Grameen Bank and its borrowing members, this joint liability system within a kinship group significantly creates peer pressure to make the payment more likely. To make such a kinship-based solidarity group by fixing a joint liability condition is hardly possible in the case of small business finance because each firm tends to be different in terms of risks and returns, and the entrepreneurs are hardly to be kin. It may also increase potential "loan shirks" as an individual member cannot perfectly watch and control the activities of other members of the group.

Thirdly, Grameen Bank charges higher interest rate and takes a weekly repayment. Such lending behavior is not viable for the small firms because it increases the mortality rate of the firms by shrinking their operating cash flows that are necessary for growth. Finally, on a legal side, microcredit institutions cannot take part in the business activities as they are not registered under the Companies Act 1994 and do

Table 6.3 Average return on investment and cost of funds for Grameen bank

Year	Average fund cost[a] (1)	Average ROL[b] (2)	Average RFD[c]	Average ROL and FD[d] (3)	Spread A= 3 − 1	Spread B= 2 − 1
2003	5.8	16.3	9.2	14.6	8.8	10.5
2004	6.2	16.7	9.1	14.7	8.5	10.5
2005	6.3	16.4	8.5	14.4	8.1	10.1
2006	7	18.4	8.6	14.8	7.8	11.4
2007	7.8	18	11.9	15.6	7.8	10.2
2008	7.8	17.1	11.4	14.9	7.1	9.3
2009	7.9	17.4	10.5	14.6	6.7	9.4
2010	8.66	18.18	12.68	17.48	8.82	9.52
2011	8.94	18.37	11.9	16.56	7.62	9.43
2012	9.04	18.08	9.12	15.86	6.82	9.04
Average	**7.54**	**17.49**	**10.29**	**15.35**	**7.80**	**9.93**

Source Authors' calculations based on Grameen Bank's financial statements, Various years

Notes

(a) Average Fund Cost = interest expense/(deposit + borrowings)

(b) Average ROL (Return on Loans) = interest on loans and advances/total loans and advances

(c) Average RFD (Return on Fixed Deposit) = interest income on FD (fixed deposit)/ total FD

(d) Average ROL and FD = interest income on both loans and FD/(loans + FD)

not pay tax on their profits. Moreover, donors often impose restrictions on the use of funds for commercial business activities.

As a whole, we find that entrepreneurial firms face a systematic problem in obtaining necessary funds from the existing financial players in Bangladesh. This is because stock markets in Bangladesh require firms to have certain asset base and profits for raising funds that the small firms do not have or cannot offer. The continual decline of stock indices, because of the involvement of some vested groups untouched by political organs, has also eroded credibility and confidence of the market even for the large firms. Bangladesh also does not have separate stock markets for promoting finance to the innovative startups and small firms.

On the other hand, commercial banks heavily rely on collaterals and use a codified system of assessing risks prescribed by the Basel principles that deter investment in uncertain startups and small firms. In furtherance of this, state-owned commercial banks and development financial institutions do not have sufficient return on assets, and they are submerged with a higher amount of NPLs that prevent them from investing in uncertain, small firms. Also, it is not advisable to direct them to extend finance to the unreliable small firms as such initiative is likely to erode their profitability further.

Similarly, the NGOs such as Grameen Bank and BRAC operate under a separate framework to give credits to the poor women, and they cannot provide credits to the small firms. The solidarity group lending approach with a weekly repayment schedule of a tiny amount of credits that NGOs practice also does not match the financial needs of the small firms.

This entire situation, in fact, shows a systematic problem in providing required credits to the entrepreneurial firms. Thus, a million dollar question is—what can be an alternative approach to financing the entrepreneurial firms? Can crowdfunding be an alternative in this respect? We tried to answer the above questions by investigating socioeconomic developments of Bangladesh and undertaking a field survey to understand the readiness of crowdfunding.

6.3 Assessing the Readiness of Crowdfunding

(i) *Socioeconomic Dynamics of Bangladesh*

A snapshot of the socioeconomic dynamics of Bangladesh is provided in Table 6.4 to understand the market readiness for crowdfunding. Table 6.4 unveils some essential features about the socioeconomic performance of Bangladesh over the last two decades on a five (5) year average scale, as follows.

First, the economy has grown at a rate of above 6% (on a five-year average scale) over the last two decades, indicating the attractiveness of the country for investment. The GDP per capita regarding PPP has increased to $2706 in 2010–14 although it had $808.25 in 1995–99. During the last two decades, inflation is also found to be

Table 6.4 Key socioeconomic indicators for Bangladesh (5-year average)

Indicator	1995–99	2000–04	2005–09	2010–14
GDP growth (%)	5.01	5.43	6.22	6.31
Per capita GDP, PPP (2005 constant US $)	808.25	953.90	1178.21	2706
Gross domestic savings (% of GDP)	14.63	17.88	16.89	20.80
Inflation (%)	6.50	4.48	7.45	7.91
Trade over GDP (%)	30.29	34.79	46.17	44.82
Agriculture, value added (% of GDP)	25.89	23.03	19.33	17
Industry, value added (% of GDP)	25.11	26.10	28.13	26.90
Services, value added (% of GDP)	49.00	50.87	52.55	56.09
Remittance (in million US $)	1424.2	2553.2	6448.2	12834
No. of stock exchanges	2	2	2	2
No. of companies listed in DSE	170	230	290	280
No. of commercial banks	49	49	48	52
Population (in million)	133.15	145.77	154.71	156.01
Working population (% of total)	57.37	59.96	61.39	64.21
Access to internets (per 100 people)	0.013	0.10	1.72	11.24
Adult literacy rate (% of people aged $\geq$15)	44.54	48.53	54.01	72.21
Human development index	0.34	0.38	0.45	0.56
CPIA (Transparency, accountability, and Corruption), 6 is the highest score	–	–	3	2.6

Source World Bank (2017) (adapted by authors), Annual Report 2015–16 (Bangladesh Bank), UNDP (2016)

bracketed within 6–8%, a level that is considered reasonable for the development of industries.

Second, the industry sector's contribution to GDP has increased over time, rising from a 25.11% in 1995–99 to 26.90 in 2010–14, although it increased to 28.13% in 2005–09. Similarly, the service sector's contribution to GDP has increased steadily from a 49% in 1995–99 to 56.09% in 2010–14. In a similar way, the trade over GDP has increased over time. However, the agriculture sector's contribution to GDP has decreased from a 25.89% in 1995–99 to 17% in 2010–14. This implies that Bangladesh economy has made a structural shift from the agriculture sector to the industry sector and service sector, and there is a demand for credits by many small business firms.

Third, the number of commercial banks that perform the main intermediary role in Bangladesh has increased from 49 in 1995–99 to 52 in 2010–14, indicating the banking sector's development in intermediating finance. The country also has an attractive gross domestic saving, 20.8% of GDP in 2010–14. The number of stock exchanges remained constant at two (2) during the same period. By contrast, the working population (as a percentage of total population) has increased from a 57.37% in 1995–99 to 68.21% in 2010–14. As a whole, this implies that although there are increased demands for funds due to the increase in socioeconomic indicators, the financial players are less prepared to meet this funding demand.

Fourth, during the last two decades, the number of internet users has dramatically increased in Bangladesh from 0.013 (per 100 people) to 11.24 in 2010–14. The adult literacy rate has also increased in a similar trend from 44.54% in 1995–99 to 72.21% in 2010–14. More importantly, the amount of remittance has increased from merely $ 1424.2 million in 1995–99 to $12834 million in 2010–14, representing the financial stability of the country for investment. The progress in these three factors, in fact, reflects the readiness of the country to adopt crowdfunding.

Finally, Bangladesh has obtained remarkable progress on the human development index (HDI)[4] over the last two decades, although it failed to improve much when transparency and corruption (CPIA) index is considered. As a whole, the socioeconomic dynamics of the country demonstrates that Bangladesh has the required readiness to grow the crowdfunding industry.

(ii) ***Survey Results for the Readiness of Crowdfunding***

To understand whether crowdfunding will be considered as a viable tool to intermediate finance to startups and small firms, we conducted a field survey in Bangladesh during August–September 2015, and February–March, 2016.[5] The survey was carried out in Bogra, Savar, Gazipur, and Khulna with a structured questionnaire using a purposive sampling device. In total, we received responses from 270 small firms of eight different categories such as agro-business, medicine and drug stores, information technology, computer service center, pathology and clinics, electronics, restaurants, and garments. We also interviewed some bank officials during August–September, 2016 to understand the awareness of crowdfunding among bank officials and the reasons for not extending sufficient credits to the small firms.[6] We selected bank officials who participated in the training programs offered by Bangladesh Institute of Bank Management in August–September, 2016. In total, we received 74 responses from different bank officials. The survey results are as follows.

(a) *Sources of Finance*

The survey reveals that 88% of the small firms obtained funds from family and relatives (47%), and NGOs and cooperatives (41%) on average, whereas only 8% of the firms received funds from banks, and 3% sought help from friends (Table 6.5).

---

[4]The HDI provides a composite measure of three basic dimensions of human development such as education, health and income (UNDP 2013)..

[5]The survey covers a very small portion of the small firms in Bangladesh. Thus, the results obtained in this survey may not represent true picture and should be used carefully..

[6]The interview covers an insignificant number of bank officials in Bangladesh compared to the total bank officials. Thus, the results obtained in this interview may not reflect true picture and should be used carefully.

Table 6.5 Sources of finance by types of firms

Types of firm	Response	Family and relatives (%)	Friend (%)	NGOs and Coop. (%)	Banks (%)	Profit (%)
Agro-business	52	54	4	35	8	0
Medicine and drug stores	54	17	6	76	2	0
Information technology	13	100	0	0	0	0
Computer service center	39	77	0	23	0	0
Pathology and clinics	22	32	0	55	14	0
Electronics	34	44	6	32	15	3
Restaurants	16	69	0	31	0	0
Garments	40	38	5	38	20	0
Total	**270**	**47**	**3**	**41**	**8**	**0**

Source authors' construction from field survey

As regards to the access to finance by types of firms, the majority of firms tend to rely on funding from family and relatives, which goes to 100% for the information and technology firms followed by computer service centers (77%), and restaurants (69%).

By contrast, NGOs tend to finance more on medicine and drug stores (76%), pathology and clinics (55%), and garments (38%) sectors. On the other hand, 20% of the garments firms received funds from banks followed by electronics (15%), and pathology and clinics (14%). Importantly, banks are found to have no finance to firms in the information technology and computer service centers. Besides, the contribution of friends and profits from business to a firm's capital is found to be very insignificant for most of the firms (Table 6.5).

(b) *Reasons for not Receiving Bank Finance*

The survey figured out several reasons for not applying or receiving finance from the commercial banks by firms (Fig. 6.2).[7] For example, nearly 35% of the firms opined that bank officers show lack of interest in providing credits to them followed by inability to offer quality tangible securities required by banks (23%). Besides, 20% of the firms think that it takes a long time to obtain credit from banks followed by a complicated procedure for credit application (18%). However, 3% of the firms believe that obtaining a loan from banks require political relationship (Fig. 6.2).

As to the types of firms, the information technology firms and restaurants think that they do not have quality tangible securities required for a bank loan, whereas firms such as pathology and clinics, electronics, agro-business, and medicine and

[7]We obtained 249 responses in this respect.

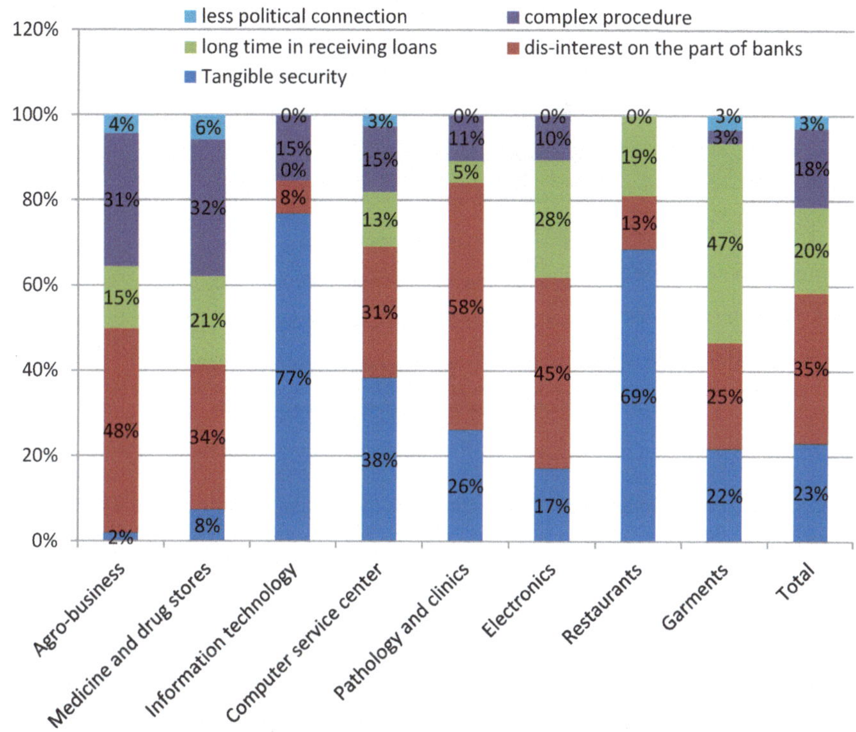

Fig. 6.2 Reasons for not receiving finance from banks by types of firms *Source* Authors' construction from field survey

drug stores cited the disinterest of the bank officials as a reason for not giving them credits. By contrast, 47% of the firms in the garments sectors believe that obtaining a loan from banks require long time followed by electronic sector (28%). Besides, 32% of the firms in medicine and drug stores, and 31% of the firms in agro-business think that obtaining credit from banks is a complicated procedure.

(c) *Awareness of Crowdfunding*

In the survey, we also checked the awareness of crowdfunding (as a mean to obtain credit) among entrepreneurs of small firms. Surprisingly, we find that on an average, only 5% of the respondents heard about the term crowdfunding, and this mainly attributes to the firms in the information technology (38%) and computer service centers (8%). However, they do not know how crowdfunding works and what they need to do in order to receive funding supports through crowdfunding platforms. Most importantly, entrepreneurs from firms such as agro-business, restaurants, and garments have never heard about crowdfunding during our survey time. As a whole, the statistic shows a very poor level of awareness of crowdfunding among small firms. These are delineated in Table 6.6.

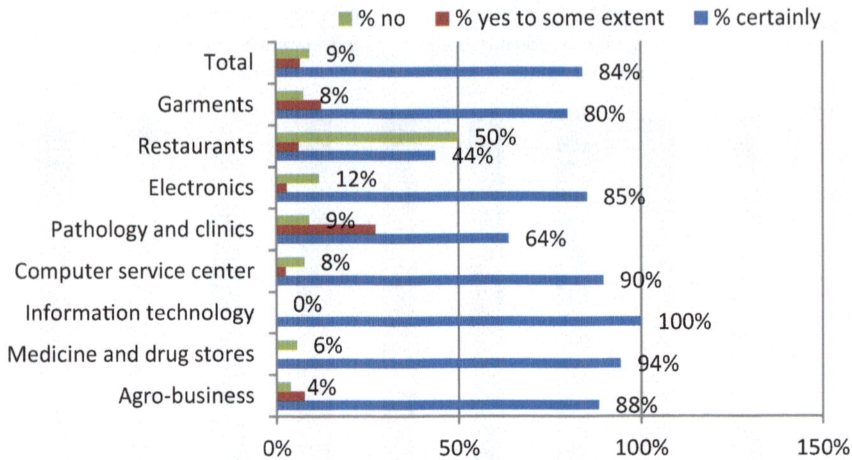

Fig. 6.3 Interest in crowdfunding by types of firms *Source* Authors' construction from field survey

(d) *Interest in Crowdfunding*

During the survey, we explained crowdfunding technology to the respondents and asked whether they felt interested in receiving financial support from crowdfunding platforms if they are built. We obtained a very positive response in this case. Figure 6.3 depicts information collected from the respondents by types of firms. As observed from Fig. 6.3, on an average, 84% of the firms are certain to use crowdfunding supports, whereas 9% may use it to some extent, and only 7% show disinterest in adopting this service. Notably, among the firms, all the respondents in the information technology claim that they are certain to use crowdfunding supports if it is available.

Table 6.6 Awareness of crowdfunding by small firms

Types of firms	No. of respondents	Yes	No	Yes (%)
Agro-business	52	0	52	0
Medicine and drug stores	54	2	52	4
Information technology	13	5	8	38
Computer service center	39	3	36	8
Pathology and clinics	22	1	21	5
Electronics	34	2	32	6
Restaurants	16	0	16	0
Garments	40	0	40	0
Total	**270**	**13**	**257**	**5**

Source author's construction from field survey

Table 6.7 Preferred types of crowdfunding by types of firms

Types of firms	Response	Donation (%)	Reward (%)	P2P (%)	Equity (%)
Agro-business	52	33	13	54	0
Medicine and drug stores	54	9	6	83	2
Information technology	13	0	0	38	62
Computer service center	39	49	0	38	13
Pathology and clinics	22	23	9	64	5
Electronics	34	6	12	65	18
Restaurants	16	0	0	100	0
Garments	40	8	0	83	10
Total	**270**	**19**	**6**	**66**	**9**

Source authors' construction from field survey

(e) *Types of Crowdfunding*

We further explained different types of crowdfunding during the survey and asked the respondents to rate a suitable one for them. The responses are summarized in Table 6.7. According to Table 6.7, on an average, 66% of the firms showed interest in P2P crowdfunding followed by donation (19%). Only 6% of the firms preferred using reward-based crowdfunding while the remaining 9% chose to use equity crowdfunding.

As regards to the choice of crowdfunding by types of firms, 100% of the firms in the restaurant sector shown to have interest in adopting P2P crowdfunding whereas no firm in the agro-business sector preferred equity crowdfunding. The donation-type crowdfunding is mostly favored by computer service firms (49%) followed by agro-business (33%), and pathology and clinics (23%). By contrast, firms under agro-business and electronics mostly like the reward-based crowdfunding, but it is not significant in terms of percentage.

(f) *Reasons for not Giving Credits to Small Firms by Banks*

We also interviewed some bank officials mentioned previously to know the reasons for not extending sufficient credits to small firms. The interview results revealed seven factors that discouraged them from providing credits to small firms. They are lack of a business plan, no cash flow projections, inadequate accounting records, insufficient collateral, higher default rates, lack of proper legal documents, and quality guarantor. Figure 6.4 shows these factors by importance.

(g) *Awareness of Crowdfunding among Bank Officials*

When asked whether bank officials are aware of crowdfunding, the survey revealed that only 9% of the bank officials know the term crowdfunding while 45% are aware of it to some extent, and the remaining 46% do not look familiar to crowdfunding. As a whole, this indicates that almost 54% of the bank officials have heard about crowdfunding, which is much higher compared to the small firms, we interviewed. Table 6.8 portrays bank officers' awareness of crowdfunding.

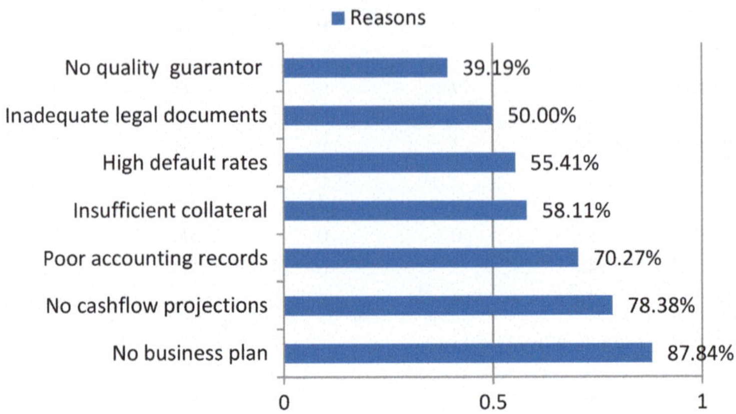

Fig. 6.4 Reasons for not giving credits by banks. *Source* Authors' construction from field survey

Table 6.8 Awareness of crowdfunding by bank officials

Bank name	Response	Yes (%)	Yes to some extent (%)	No (%)
Sonali Bank	11	9	64	27
Rupali Bank	3	0	67	33
Agrani Bank	9	11	33	56
Janata Bank	7	14	57	29
Shahjalal Islami Bank	3	0	67	33
Southeast Bank	7	14	14	71
Uttara Bank	4	25	25	50
NCC Bank	3	0	33	67
NRBCB Bank	2	0	50	50
Woori Bank	1	0	0	100
Prime Bank	6	17	33	50
Trust Bank	5	0	40	60
United Commercial	3	33	33	33
Al-Arafah Islami Bank	4	0	75	25
EXIM Bank	4	0	50	50
IFIC Bank	2	0	50	50
Total	**74**	**9**	**45**	**46**

Source authors' construction from field survey

(h) *Suggestions for the Development of Crowdfunding in Bangladesh*

During the interview, we further asked both the bank officials and entrepreneurs of small firms to list out possible ways to implement the crowdfunding technology in Bangladesh. We obtained following suggestions from them, as follows.

- It is essential to ensure trust and security in the operation of crowdfunding platforms by formulating necessary laws and regulations.
- More information is needed on Japan's crowdfunding model and its success.
- NGOs can be incorporated into the crowdfunding model in Bangladesh.
- Bank can open a separate window to offer crowdfunding service.
- Islamic Banks can create a CFP taking a portion of Zakat money as a case.
- Trade bodies such as DCCI, FBCCI, and AMCHAMBD should offer crowdfunding service.
- Bangladesh Bank and Ministry of Finance should take the initiative to familiarize crowdfunding.
- World Bank and USAID should provide initial support to set up the crowdfunding industry.
- Bangladesh Telecommunications authority should increase the speed of internet and make it affordable as the success of crowdfunding depends on the speed and use of internets.

In sum, our survey reveals several important issues regarding the funding supports to the small firms and introduction to crowdfunding as an alternative option. First, most of the small firms in Bangladesh tend to obtain funds from family and relatives followed by NGOs and cooperatives, indicating a lack of access to bank finance and a shortage of growth capital for them as well. Second, the funding problem is found to be very high for firms in the information and technology sector and computer service centers as they are unable to offer quality real securities required for a bank loan. Third, most of the small firms believe that bank officials have little interest to give them credits, and hence, they adopt complex procedures for giving credits.

Fourth, and by contrast, bank officials note that small firms do not receive sufficient credits because of lack of business plan followed by poor accounting records, insufficient collateral, inadequate legal documents, higher default rates, and failure to provide a quality guarantor, indicating a perceived mismatch between entrepreneurs of small firms and bank officials. Fifth, the awareness of crowdfunding among entrepreneurs of small firms is indeed very poor although bank officials have relatively a higher level of knowledge in this respect. However, bank officials tend to prefer the use of existing loan products to provide funding support to the small firms although some of them argued that bank can open a separate window to introduce crowdfunding service. Finally, most of the small firms like to use P2P-type crowdfunding over equity crowdfunding, perhaps, because of the fear to lose control of their business.

So, can crowdfunding be an alternative option to cater to the financing needs of the small firms in Bangladesh? We argue positively to this point. We found that small firms in Bangladesh are systematically omitted from the attention of the traditional financial players such as banks, stock markets, and NGOs, and the country needs to ensure available finance for them to continue its GDP growth rate. The country also exhibits socioeconomic attractiveness in terms GDP growth rates, flows of remittances, size of the population, and increased access to mobile and internets. In the above setup, with proper support from the government and other trade bodies, crowdfunding can solve much of the funding problems for the small firms in Bangladesh and can further increase the country's ability to leapfrog its capital market structures similar to the developed world.

However, regarding the choice of model, it is difficult to figure out which type of crowdfunding models would be suitable for Bangladesh, as all the crowdfunding models have both merits and demerits. At the introduction stage, a guaranteed return model under the ambit of financial return framework (say, P2P model) could be a suitable one, as the country does not have impressive outlook regarding transparency and corruption index. Notably, Muslims constitute almost 92% of the population in Bangladesh. On a religious rule, they pay Zakat—a donation of their income to the poor people—each year and this Zakat money could be used to form a donation-based or equity-based crowdfunding model, as interest is prohibited in Islam.

A notable example in this regard could be Eureeca (www.eureeca.com), a Lebanese Islamic finance-compliant site that has created an incubator-based model that profoundly embeds equity crowdfunding to accredited investors and does not release specific data. Their first campaign raised US$100,000 from 23 investors. To continue, Bangladesh has a total number of eight (8) Islamic Banks that can take the pioneering role in this regard. Besides, a proper understanding of the crowdfunding ecosystem (discussed in Sect. 6.4) is essential to the successful implantation of this new technology.

6.4 Designing a Crowdfunding Ecosystem

Crowdfunding is a recent phenomenon. The adoption of crowdfunding requires proper understanding of the crowdfunding ecosystem. The credibility of a crowdfunding ecosystem depends not only to the willingness of the investors, people involved in setting up crowdfunding platforms, and entrepreneurs but also supports from prudential regulations and communities and interest of the government to promote technology ventures. A credible crowdfunding platform requires giving value to religious, cultural, emotional and spiritual attachment of society to accommodate a new financial tool like crowdfunding. In other words, the "constellation of trust" by involving participation from all stakeholders is indeed essential to create a robust crowdfunding ecosystem (World Bank 2013). The key factors that have contributed to the development of crowdfunding in Western countries include:

(i) A vibrant regulatory framework that would ensure proper protection to all stakeholders associated with crowdfunding. Due to the advancement of internet technology, regulators can adopt an array of new tools to protect investors.

Regulators can also work for hand in hand with the technology companies and innovative firms to detect fraud and to monitor crowdfunding platforms.

(ii) A substantial penetration into the social media market and widespread Internet usage that is necessary to tap into demographic and technology trends to bring about collaboration and cultural shifts (World Bank 2013). The success of crowdfunding largely depends on the ability to efficiently tap into the potential of the social media to broaden the reach of the fundraising campaigns, provide tools for better measurement of risks, and reduce the friction in the process of raising capital.

(iii) An online marketplace that is regulated but one that at the same time facilitates capital generation while providing the investor enough protection through education and training. Regulators can utilize equity and debt-based crowdfunding and offer better protection to investors than they could have ever done in an offline world. Capital formation online creates the opportunity to monitor and report on what both entrepreneurs and investors are doing on these online platforms in ways never before possible. The power of the crowd is also harnessed for additional diligence and real-time monitoring of campaigns

(iv) Collaboration with other entrepreneurial events and hubs including business plan competitions, incubators, accelerators, universities and co-working places to open channels for opportunities and oversight (World Bank 2013). There is an opportunity to look at new ways to structure these entities and their activities to take advantage of the ways that crowdfunding can support these processes, including issues such as product market fit, entrepreneurial execution, and fundraising execution.

(v) Moreover, the collaborative power of crowdfunding is a result of a few deeper and more meaningful relationships coming together to a business or a team. As the smaller and tightly connected first-level-connection group gives their public support and dollars to business, others see that as a signal and follow along, further amplifying the fundraiser. In short, big networks are always not the key to successful fundraising.

Figure 6.5 shows critical factors for building a crowdfunding ecosystem. As Fig. 6.5 indicates, the key stimuli of the crowdfunding system are the access opportunities to viral networks, peoples' willingness to participate in the system or entrepreneurial spirit of the country (culture), and assurance of confidence in the system by enabling higher internet security and formulating some basic laws and regulations to safeguard investors.

Notably, at the initial stage, it is the responsibility of the government to ensure the existence of above factors. The government also needs to create a congenial atmosphere to provide supports for co-working spaces, incubators and accelerators to foster an entrepreneurial culture. Simultaneously, crowdfunding platforms (CFPs) need to ensure transparency and accountability in their operations to build trust and confidence in the minds of the fund suppliers as well as social communities. CFPs also need to disclose funding activities through online and maintain close relationships with business firms and local banks to make the system vibrant, credible, and sustainable.

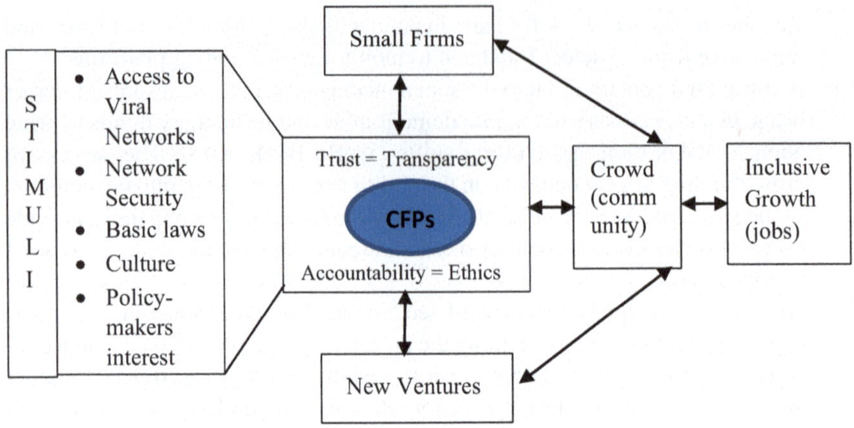

Fig. 6.5 Crowdfunding ecosystem *Source* Authors' construction

References

Bangladesh Bank (2016). Annual report 2015–16. Bangladesh Bank

Hoff K, Stiglitz J (1990) Imperfect information and rural credit markets: puzzles and policy perspectives. The World Bank Economic Review 4(3):235–250

Ministry of Finance (2010) The industrial policy 2010. Ministry of Finance, Bangladesh

Stiglitz J, Weiss A (1981) Credit rationing in markets with imperfect information. Am Econ Rev 71(3):393–410

World Bank (2013) Crowdfunding potentials for the developing world. InfoDev, Finance and Private Sector Development, Washington D.C

World Bank (2017). World Development Indicators

UNDP (2017) 2016 Human development report. Accessed Sept 2017. http://hdr.undp.org/en/countries/profiles/BGD

Chapter 7
Lessons of Crowdfunding

Crowdfunding is a new phenomenon in market-based finance. It falls under the ambit of modern entrepreneurial finance. It leverages social media and information technology to intermediate finance to those are in need of it, startups and idea creators, in particular. However, it is neither microfinance nor micro-investment. It is web-based finance supplied by a large pool of investors, and the amount of fund depends on the needs of the entrepreneurs. Crowdfunding fills the gap of financing uncared by the microcredit institutions and commercial banks. It does not replace the angel investors and venture capitalists. Instead, it serves as a compliment to them. The critical stimuli of the crowdfunding system are the access opportunities to viral networks, peoples' willingness to participate in the system (culture), and assurance of confidence in the system by enabling higher internet security mechanisms and formulating prudential laws.

The birth of social media and advancement information technology (Web 2.0) has been critical to the evolution, diffusion, and growth of crowdfunding technology worldwide. The size of the crowdfunding industry reached to US $34.4 billion in 2015, and it expects to reach nearly US $187 billion including peer-to-peer (P2P) lending in 2021 (statistia.com, 2017). The equity-based crowdfunding has been the latest phenomenon to provide a complement or substitute for seed financing which expects to reach $36 billion by 2020, showing a tendency to surpass the venture capital industry as a significant source of finance for startups. The ad hoc regulations in many countries, especially for P2P type crowdfunding, tend to augment the growth of the industry further. However, the real growth of the industry would be known when this instrument becomes more regulated and legitimized.

Crowdfunding reduces much of screening problem associated with entrepreneurial finance as the crowdfunding platform, and a large number of potential investors with diverse backgrounds does the screening. However, the success of a proposal depends mostly on the entrepreneur's ability, commitment, and sincerity in the post-fund utilization stage. This raises problems of moral hazard and agency problem as well. To solve the moral hazard problem, crowdfunding platforms tend to ask fundraisers to present the post-fund performance on the

B. K. Adhikary et al., *Crowdfunding*, SpringerBriefs in Economics,
https://doi.org/10.1007/978-981-13-1522-0_7

crowdfunding platforms on a timely basis (quarterly or bi-annually). In some cases, crowdfunding platforms use conditional payment technique (funds will be mobilized step by steps) to reduce investors 'moral hazard. However, it does not reduce entrepreneurs' moral hazard and incentive problem. Thus, the growth of crowdfunding in the future is likely to depend on how the agency problem or for that matter the governance of the capital seeking firms will be addressed.

Crowdfunding is largely used for financing young startups and incubation of new technologies. However, getting good creators or entrepreneurs would likely to be a big issue in the future as there are ample instances where projects posted for crowdfunding have not been successful. In the case of Japan, the crowdfunding models tend to follow a relationship or community-based approach backed by stakeholder theory. This approach integrates local banks, trade bodies, and government officials from the City Office to solicit viable candidates for crowdfunding with a long-term view. Besides, it reduces screening problem and investors' moral hazard. Thus, the Japanese crowdfunding technique could be suitable for receiving good firms for crowdfunding in developing countries such as Bangladesh. Notably, Bangladesh has a number of NGOs and cooperatives that provide finance to the rural market, and if a business link is created with them, they could be an influential player to recommend viable candidates for crowdfunding.

In every society, some people tend to have brilliant ideas, but they fail to translate them into reality because of the lack of knowledge in preparing an action-oriented business plan. This implies that the government should provide incentives to technology and science researchers', and simultaneously promote entrepreneurial education institute to ensure the supply of brilliant entrepreneurs for crowdfunding. Undoubtedly, the sustainability of crowdfunding depends on the supply of new and innovative entrepreneurs.

The involvement of venture capitalists and business angles with the crowdfunding technology would be likely to spur crowdfunding as this expects to improve the governance quality of the crowdfund-backed firms, thereby reducing the investor's moral hazard. Industry clustering and the creation of entrepreneurial database may further serve as a lubricant to crowdfunding.

It is said that people are by nature not a thief but opportunity makes them be a thief. This indicates that although the "trust" is viewed as one of the foundations of crowdfunding, it is very fragile in societies that have higher chances of opportunism. Therefore, to safeguard crowdfunding industry from potential shirks, the government needs to enact prudential laws and regulations for the crowdfunding platforms.

Crowdfunding is mostly an internet phenomenon that is not free from cyber-attack and other fraudulent activities such as money laundering and terrorism financing. Therefore, government and individual crowdfunding platform should check such threats and dishonest practices by adopting appropriate mechanism through continuously interacting with technology organizations.

Crowdfunding is used for financing the small firms and technology incubators which tend to have higher mortality rates. Thus, investors may lose capital in the absence of proper risk mitigating techniques. This implies that the policy-making institutions must institute proper risk mitigating techniques to make the industry successful. One of the mitigating risk methods could be to build an "investors protection fund" by taking a flat rate on the funds raised by the firms through CFPs.

Now, crowdfunding is used to finance not only the startups and idea creators but also the matured industries such as real estate and construction firms. Therefore, crowdfunding may pose a threat to the technology financing markets such as Mothers, Hercules, NASDAQ, and ChiNext. It may also raise conflicts of interest with the principal stock markets such as Tokyo Stock Exchange, and Tokyo Stock Exchange.

It is highly likely that shortly crowdfund-seekers would use hybrid financial instruments (instruments that combine both debt and equity features). Crowdfunding platforms may also link platforms assets with the principal financial markets to create derivate securities to expand their operations. This indicates that the crowdfunding industry would likely be divergent and undergo through the strict regulatory framework.

From the perspective of a developing country, crowdfunding is still relatively new although spreading across borders quickly, and the potential for mobilizing crowdfunding in the developing world could be significant for the support of innovation, growth, and jobs. Capitalization on this opportunity will necessitate the creation of a learning curve about factors required for successful crowdfunding as experienced in the developed world.

This new financial technology could be a powerful tool to cater to the financing needs of the small firms in developing countries especially for the small firms in Bangladesh that are systematically missed out form the attention of the traditional financial players. Bangladesh also exhibits potential for crowdfunding in terms of its GDP growth rates, flows of remittances, size of the population, and increased access to mobile and internet communications. It can further improve the country's ability to leapfrog its capital market structures similar to the developed world. Thus, with proper support from the government and local banks, crowdfunding can play the work of wonder in Bangladesh.

Crowdfunding has the potential to play several essential roles in the developing worlds' entrepreneurial and venture finance ecosystem. However, compared with the developed world, many developing countries are challenged by some cultural, economic, and institutional forces that have suppressed entrepreneurial activity and funding. Nevertheless, there is considerable potential for crowdfunding investment platforms to channel individual savings in developing countries to projects within their own city, country, or region. Crowdfund investment platforms, therefore, have the potential to provide returns to individual investors, change societal norms, return capital to a home country, and provide investment opportunities to channel savings as well as generate wealth, innovation, and jobs.

Crowdfunding depends upon and finds inspiration from other innovations that have helped shape enterprise in the developing world. Several examples show the potential for new technology and models to be adapted to cultivate the spirit of innovation and entrepreneurship despite the many challenges faced by the developing world. Many of these initiatives have succeeded in installing a better model than the one existing in the developed world. Among the many examples worth mentioning are the mobile payments in East Africa, low-cost drip irrigation in India and alternative fuel adoption (ethanol) in Brazil.

While just beginning to engage in crowdfunding, the developing world is also showing signs of early adoption. The rise in the number of crowdfunding platforms and utilization of these platforms is related to a number of factors that vary by region. In the developing world, crowdfunding is still is in the embryonic stage. Therefore, most of the early campaign successes are not found in high-growth technology focussed entrepreneurial ventures. Instead, early campaigns have concentrated on raising money for artistic and cause-related issues. These artistic and cause-related issues may be seen as the "green shoots" that lead to entrepreneurial engagement in crowdfunding. This phenomenon was also seen in the developed world—at first artistic and cause campaigns used crowdfunding and then entrepreneurs woke up to the idea of crowdfunding as a new channel to sell inventory and raise equity and debt capital.

It is noteworthy that the first significant crowdfunding platform in the developed world was founded in 2008; just two to three years before developing nations began to establish crowdfunding platforms. Given such a short head start, innovators and entrepreneurs in developing countries are moving quickly to both adapt existing models as well as create new models to utilize the processes and game mechanics of crowdfunding and crowdfund investing.

As in the developed world, the suitability of crowdfunding for projects or high-growth entrepreneurs will depend on the project or business type, geographic presence, and the funding required. The type of crowdfunding that could be appropriate for a given project depends on the type of project and its capital needs. Donation-based crowdfunding is most applicable to art or community-related projects, microfinance to micro development, social lending to cash flow-based credit to small enterprises, and crowdfund investing to high-growth and technology-focused entrepreneurs. Equity crowdfunding applies to businesses that have a sale, merger, or IPO strategy. Debt crowdfunding is more suitable to businesses that do not have a sale strategy, need short-term cash and have the cash flow to pay off the debt.

The level of foreign direct investment appears to be related to the launch of crowdfunding in a country. A second related variable is the amount of remittances flowing into a country coming from its citizens living outside the parent country. Though additional research is needed, early findings indicate that crowdfunding may both reflect the interest of the international community to invest in a given country, and serve as a mechanism for remittance capital to be deployed into high-growth potential companies to further economic expansion in a country.

Crowdfunding may provide a financial outlet for diaspora members' emotional desires to strengthen their country or population of origin. The term diaspora refers to the dispersion of people who share a common ethnicity from their homeland. Membership of a particular diaspora group typically is based on original nation-state, religious, regional, ethnolinguistic, or other identifying criteria, to which members have retained their emotional, cultural, and spiritual links. Belonging to a diaspora entails a consciousness of, and emotional attachment to, commonly claimed origins and cultural attributes. Sites such as HomeStrings.com have demonstrated the ability for web-based donor platforms to channel diaspora investments back to a country. The growth of crowdfunding in the developing world may be influenced by these dynamics and could give rise to regionally specific crowdfunding platforms that attract donations or investments from the diaspora community.

Indeed, crowdfunding in the developing world provides an opportunity to study remittance and diaspora capital flows with the goal of discovering best practice and encouraging greater investment from former citizens or residents. Governments may consider the benefits of remittance dollars flowing through crowdfunding platforms, which provide a digital footprint of the money flows. These digital footprints can help governments understand more about the financial health and level of commitment to their country among members of the country's diaspora. Crowdfunding platforms can identify the current country of residence of a funder, the types of companies/entrepreneurs that diaspora investors are funding and the level of commitments from those funders.

Last, but not the least, the development of a credible crowdfunding ecosystem requires more than entrepreneurs and willing investors. Supportive factors include, *inter alia*, forward-thinking regulations, effective technological solutions, influential social media, and regulated online markets. Furthermore, accumulation of knowledge continually being with the developed economies is indeed essential to make the crowdfunding ecosystem more effective and appropriate for country needs.

The manufacturer's authorised representative in the EU is Springer Nature Customer Service Centre GmbH, Europaplatz 3, 69115 Heidelberg, Germany. If you have any concerns regarding our products, please contact ProductSafety@springernature.com

Printed and bound by CPI Group (UK) Ltd, Croydon, CR0 4YY
22/09/2026
02220981-0018